To Al

Thank you for spending
time with me and
making Trainfest more fun!
Enjoy my book!

— Cidafrey

AMERICA,
CAN I HAVE YOUR
AUTOGRAPH?
The Story of Junior Ranger Aida Frey

Aida Frey and Dana Dorfman

A BOOK THAT GIVES KIDS A GREAT DAY!

Excitement's secret formula lies in a kid from Chicago, Aida Frey, nicknamed, Ranger. She has all but cartwheeled through her pages! Exciting and thrilling, her personally written notes about her Two Hundred National Park Friendship Tour is a colossal event and a reading extravaganza that blasts kids to extraordinary places that exist but may never have been imagined! It is like sitting down in a Cineplex with a big box of buttery popcorn to watch the latest box office smash except there are no caped figures or glittery explosions or other Hollywood effects. Instead, the superheroes are America's national parks, wildlife, nature and fascinating adventures of America herself! Aida Frey's travel narrative is all about KID FUN and friendship! Every page is a life sweeping adventure as kids are taken down to the depths of the earth, travel back through the passages of time and ushered to the steps of The White House!

Aida's tree-loving travels, wild animal adventures and cave explorations are wowing kids all over the nation with a new kind of kid fun! Her Two Hundred National Parks Friendship Tour in four years and her 2-gun salute in her honor at Allegheny Portage Railroad National Historic Site plus her Aida Day at Effigy Mounds and her travels to The Sears Tower, John Dillinger Museum, Michael Jackson House, Graceland and the Elvis Presley Birthplace are one-of-a-kind travels. But it is Aida's amazing interviews with national park rangers and superintendents, as well as her wonderful trip to Tupelo, Mississippi and her interview with Mayor Shelton spotlights her book and is among the many fireworks that light up her pages!

The amazing fun power of this book increases a kid's confidence and glitters their lives with positive thoughts! Their voices come alive with excitement! This book makes kids feel respected! The one-size-fits-all attitude of these pages gives kids a brand new sense of self. This book is a rocket of kid confidence and is filled with friendship insight. These fun-filled pages are a first-place finish! America Can I Have Your Autograph, The Story of Junior Ranger Aida Frey will fill everyone who reads it with fun, laughter, and out of this world enjoyment!

Never before does a book have the bells and whistles to make you feel like you are at a party; the pages are so filled with grins! So get ready to have an amazing time! Expect to be dazzled! Release the balloons! Throw the confetti! America Can I Have Your Autograph, The Story of Junior Ranger Aida Frey makes kids happy! It is a wow event for the entire family that shows just what can happen when a kid and their country become best friends!

BIOGRAPHER'S NOTE

Aida, your book is like opening up a drawer that is overflowing with fun! Written in the glitter of friendship, it is filled with loads of laughter and tons of a kid's smiles and grins! Confetti seems to fall on every page and I find myself wishing that every kid in the world has the pleasure of reading your book and smiling as brightly as you do.

I like where you imagine a future world where kids are kindly to each other and treated with respect by the world. I like the way in which you eavesdrop on your fears and hopes and the beautiful way you convey to your fellow kids to have and achieve fascinating goals! There is no doubt that this book is about a new kind of kid power and contains the secret formula for being a good friend and having fun! It is about giving kids respect!

Kids and grownups live with the everydayness of school and work, cellphones, texting, email, movies, the computer and TV. Every once in a blue moon something comes along that is magically different, so magically different that it stuns the world in a magnificent way. Such is the story of you, Junior Ranger Aida Frey, an ordinary girl from Chicago! The beautiful reality of your book is that it shows the world how to treat kids with respect. If they are treated with respect, then they will treat each other with respect! Aida your book shows this and so much more!

Aida, your admiration for America's national parks is the basis of your book and is the new kid power of this nation; it is the new kid fun! But it is your friendships that spark the breaths of your magnificent travels. Through your travels your book teaches kids how to have fun and gives kids the secret formula for being a great friend. Aida, your book makes a kid feel good. The social support of family is apparent in your story as is the importance of having a good time with your family and friends. It also teaches kids how to appreciate the cool stuff in America and America's history. The family dynamic that has been discovered in your story has the secret formula for changing the world and holds the secret of making kids feel important. Aida, your book is a growing learning stop for kids and adults.

When your family first came to me to write your book, they came to me with this delightful sense of warmth that made me feel as if I had known them! We didn't really know how this book would turn out. We were pursuing so many lines of thinking, but I knew from the very beginning, Aida, that your book would no doubt be something special. Aida, you are a shining example of a breath of fresh air! You are the twirl in the rain and the shimmer around the trees. I am not one to stitch pretty words together when I write someone's biography, but your pages break through the clouds with a story that just can't be more beautiful. Aida, you have gallantly made your way through history and the national park world. Your book teaches kids how to have fun and how to be a great friend.

Aida, your book is an ambitious book full of personal adventure and travel. In your pages is your attempt to connect the dots of history and open up a path for kids all over the country to experience their personal triumphs and solve some mysteries of the world. I don't know, Aida, but after writing your pages, I cannot help but feel your passion, curiosity and zeal are what hold the key to understanding civilization! Your friendship lessons give kids and adults a can-do-attitude that make us all feel like first place winners! You seem to have a knack for friendship that I have never seen before. Your values of the world are stunning. You are a master storyteller. I felt like I was there throughout your entire national park journey. More than anything Aida, you are likable. You are so very likable. I like your buddy nature and your dream that everyone in the world can be friends. I think that you hold the key for making this come true. If kids could have a leader you would be the choice! If you were a kid ambassador, you would bring every kid in the world happiness and they would live under ballooned skies and on confetti streets!

A special thank you to your parents Norma and Shawn Frey and of course to you my dear friend Aida! You have a keen grasp on how to make the world better. I love your travels and your discoveries! You are filled with some of the greatest stories I have ever heard. I admire your unlimited energy and how you use enthusiasm as your way to self-discovery. Sometimes I think you are so crammed with enthusiasm that you will pop like a brightly-colored giant balloon! You, my dear friend Aida, you send all the right moral messages out to the world in a book of totally cool stuff! You have a book that creates carefree days that are not easily forgotten.

Lastly, your book is such a powerful force. It is stirred by your enthusiasm and your life inside this book! You are filled with such excitement! Your spirit, alone, will change a kid's life. It will bring a new sense of living and laughing to kids. I also like the way you and your family have brought back a vanishing way of life: car travel. I like your peanut butter sandwiches, sliced apples with peanut butter, your vampire teeth and your feet painting! You are an extensively illustrated account of good ol' kid fun! I love it and I loved writing your book! Everyone who reads this book should value their silliness and learn to be unafraid and to take chances. I would be proud to download your book or have it on my shelf!

May your happiness and passion touch everyone who reads it and may the glow of your pages artfully paint your life in America's national parks!

I am honored to be your biographer. I am honored to be your friend.

Dana Dorfman

Hello Everybody!

I am Junior Ranger Aida Frey. I want to welcome everyone to my book! It is about fun, friendship and how kids can be great friends to each other, to their parents, their families and to themselves. It is inspired by my love for America's national parks, my cool stops along the way and the friendship I have found with my country. Friendship is magic. And so, my book begins in the magical heart of my amazing adventure. It is about my Two Hundred National Park Friendship Tour, amazing cool stuff and my amazing life as a kid!

My Two Hundred National Park Friendship Tour has introduced me to so many amazing experiences. I really feel as if I have broken out of the ordinary everyday stuff in life! I meet new people and see new sights. Of course sometimes I doze off in the backseat as we are driving to these fascinating places but it is all part of my life as a kid!

It is fun to go wildlife watching and nature exploring! It is amazing to visit caves and see things you don't see every single day! Sometimes we visit places and just follow the cobblestones! I just love when we do that! I like just being so carefree and following the breadcrumbs of life! It makes me feel so alive! I love when my dad just does that! He will just follow a sign whose destination sounds fun and we just go there! I love not being on a schedule! It makes you feel so good and so free and that all you have on your schedule is fun and enjoyment! I believe that everyone needs this in their life! That is what vacationing is all about! This is what living is all about!

I never know what we are going to come across and it is so exciting! What is the energy across the other side of the road! What kind of story am I going to tell my friends when I get home! What will I learn that I don't know! I am always coming across new things. America is filled with awesome stuff! There is a world to see in America! It is interesting to learn about different cultures and the way life was. I like seeing and learning about everything that was. It is a way to connect with past generations and to explore and discover cool stuff!

I think storytelling is really important in a kid's life. It is fun to be able to tell your friends about your vacations, things you do and things you see in life. It is fascinating to explore and experience what other kids do. It is amazing to hear what kids wish for and their lessons of life. Listening to kids tell their stories helps kids listen better to their friends, develop their concentration skills, have a great attitude and just talk better because they feel great about themselves! Kids and their conversations improve from storytelling. I think kids better understand each other by listening to one another's stories. We are all part of everything that was and everything that is!

Making friends is so important. I have learned so much in my journey as a kid. I have learned what friendship means to me, how to make friends and that friendship can be so magical! We all have our own buddy nature. Some kids have a quiet buddy nature about them and you are not sure if they want you to be their friend. Other kids are really outgoing and talk a lot and they make it known that they want to be your friend. I really do believe that every kid has their own particular type of friendship to offer.

I hope that my book inspires kids to visit America's national parks and talk about their experiences. Visiting America's national parks is a life-changing experience. Visiting the cool stops along the way is a life-changing experience too! The visits make for great conversations, help you to meet new people (the rangers and superintendents at the parks are great people) and have so many stories about the national parks and about history! The national parks encourage kids in so many great ways to learn and live. I really do think that kids and grownups love a great story. Yes! Everyone loves a great story!

I am honored to have so many wonderful people step into my pages and be part of it all! A special thanks to everyone! I hope you enjoy my book. I have written it personally to kids all over the world. It is a book of friendship notes and pages filled with my amazing adventures! It is filled with great stories, lots of fun and the secret formula for building great friendships and tips for being the best friend ever! I hope my pages make it into the hearts of everyone!

My road trip to America's national parks and other cool stuff along the way is at times like a road-trip buddy film. It is definitely not boring! My parents can really be a riot and there are so many things that we see that make us just crack up in the car. Take the time we pulled into this rest stop area and there was this kid who had this huge Mohawk hairstyle. I mean it was huge. My dad thought it would be a riot if this kid would take a picture with me. It was like a skit seeing my dad running after this kid with his camera. The hairstyle really was creative the way he did it and it just ended up being another chapter in our travel-buddy film! My dad never did get to catch up with him to snap a picture but it did make for a great car conversation and for many chuckles along the way to our adventures!

I want to tell kids everywhere something! Don't let your kid life just pass you by! Life is exciting! Discover your own story, get off of the couch, do something outdoors! Disconnect from the internet and experience new things! Meet new people! Experience the wonders of America's national parks! It is fun to be best friends with your country!

Thank you everyone! To friendship!!

Your New Friend,
Aida

P.S. One more thing! I am a 2038 Presidential hopeful! So, remember me!

Get Used To Succeeding In Life
And You Will Never Be Bored!

Aida Frey

THE ALLEGHENY PORTAGE RAILROAD NATIONAL HISTORIC SITE

Gallitzin Township, PA

Boom! Boom!

I felt a rumbling beneath my feet! My toes rattled! It was like an exploding burst of thunder. Mesmerized, my eyes grew wider and wider. I couldn't turn away from what was happening. The two gunners dotted with black top hats raised their muskets. It was not a dream. Oh no! It was real! It was as if everything glittered in my view and I was a glowing figure of happiness! It was my 2-gun salute at Allegheny Portage Railroad National Historic Site! It was amazing! It was as if I had rubbed a magic lamp and my life swirled into a crash of symbols and an orchestra of pipes and drums. And then it was like a big gigantic smile illuminated the sky! It is in this giant smile I tell my story.

It was a yummy day in Pennsylvania! The prettiest vanilla cake you ever saw topped with layers of vanilla frosting welcomed my parents and me as we pulled into Allegheny filling us with sweet surprise! I couldn't believe it! I really couldn't! My tummy was tumbling! You see, The Allegheny Portage Railroad National Historic Site was my 200th park in my four year journey of seeing America's national parks and it was a very big day in my life! I was being honored with a two-gun salute along with a beautiful cake reception and I was beyond excited!

Ships sail into harbors and receive gun salutes! Gun salutes are for princes and kings and queens! They are for presidents of nations and dignitaries and they also honor someone or are in honor of something such as a great occasion. In modern times gun salutes are also sendoffs to departing directors who have gone beyond their calling. The tradition goes way back and is an ancient naval tradition. The 21-gun salute was adopted as the standard salute for royalty in 1808. So it was my 200th National Park Anniversary, and you may be wondering just what does that mean? You see, I have travelled to 200 national parks in four years and that is awesome! Not bad for a fourteen year old kid to have a 2-gun salute in her kid career! So I am being celebrated today and it is a very big moment for me and of course for my parents! Let me talk a bit about Allegheny because this place is pretty awesome.

The Allegheny Portage Railroad National Historic Site is just a hop, skip and a jump from Johnstown Flood and some of the rangers at Johnstown Flood also work at Allegheny. They have become good friends! Visiting so many national parks, I have made so many friends along the way! It seems like wherever I go, I know someone who remembers me and I remember them. It is just such an awesome feeling. People are shaking my hand and smiling at me and some are asking for my autograph. Can you imagine? But I have also gotten to know myself along the way too! Accomplishing something you set out to do is a great feeling! There is nothing like it! Really! I love the feeling of success.

Bunches of years ago, way before I was born, railroad technology was born! The flatbed railroad cars loaded with cargo along with passengers was breaking the travel barrier and cutting travel time from weeks to days! Tunneling through mountains railroad travel increased the speed of moving! The Portage Railroad officially opened March 18, 1834 and when this happened it became possible to travel from Philadelphia to Pittsburgh in about four days. It ran for twenty years and I could only think that this train was the superstar of the day! But there was more! Interestingly, Allegheny Portage Railroad holds a big place in America's history and a big place in my history. Because, it is here where I will receive a two gun salute in my honor! And do you know something? I can already feel that this is going to be an amazing memory for me! You know as a kid how you can just feel things sometimes?

The Allegheny Portage Railroad National Historic Site tells a story when you see it. It is a story of forests and fields and mountains, and it has an outdoorsy prettiness about it that is so awesome! The Visitor

Center is done in stone and is just beautiful. Everything has an old brick colonial feel to it and I it is like I am in another time. Standing on the old railroad tracks, I feel like if I stand here long enough I will hear the train chugging along and will have to jump out of the way! I can almost see the train engineer waving his stove piped hat at me as it chugs its way along making history!

My beautiful vanilla cake with white frosting awaits me in The Visitors Center. I am so excited about this. I really don't even know what to expect! Walking in the reception room, I see many rangers are here, some even from Johnstown Flood! Wow! It is just an out-of-this-world feeling! Wow! It is like I am being welcomed by a room full of friends! I really don't know how else to describe it!

Adventures make up history and this adventure of mine is part of my history as a kid! You know, us kids have history! When you accomplish something it just makes you remember that day in time and how important it is and how important it continues to be. I keep a souvenir diary of all of the places I've been and all the souvenirs I pick up along the way. I even keep tickets to places! It helps me to remember it all!

My eyes are as wide as they can be in anticipation! The rangers are all around me as I read the words on my cake: Happy 200th Park Aida! Oh wow! And I am the happiest fourteen year old girl on the planet. I didn't want to eat it because it was just too important to eat! But, I did! Everyone was eating and it was wonderful and then the rangers all got up. My parents and I got up and we followed them. I knew it was time for my two-gun salute. I don't think I have ever felt so respected and so important in all my life! You know, respect is a very interesting thing. It can totally change your outlook on life. I think kids should be respected for things that they do and recognized for it. Going to school and getting good grades is a reason to be recognized and respected. But, making friends and giving recognition and respect to your friends is really important. I think that a way for kids to gain respect from each other is through storytelling. I am telling my story in this book. When you tell a story and others listen to you or read about you, they are giving you respect. Respect feels good!

And so we leave the Visitors Center and I am happy. I am happy and red faced as I feel the freezing cold of the day blowing my hair. I am cold but I am warm inside! I feel proud. I am filled with such an amazing feeling and I realize something. Always amaze yourself in life and be filled with ambition! It is the key to feeling awesome! Do things in life and be proud of all that you do! You know, us kids have the ability to move the earth!

My parents and I make our way to the tavern area and it is getting colder! Putting up our hoods, I see two men dressed in 19th century garb. They are wearing black top hats and grey coats. They have little knapsacks and they are holding really old fashioned guns, like long barrel muskets. I take a really long look at them. I want to remember their every move. I don't want to forget a thing, especially the small American flags, affixed in the ground, blowing softly in the wind.

Guns pressed against their chests, they are straight-faced, expressionless. I stare at the scene before me. And then the men in grey coats turn away from me. My heart is pounding. Loading their guns, I watch them closely. I wish I could catch a glimpse of myself right now and see the excitement in my eyes! I can't take my eyes off of what I am seeing. It is so amazing. I don't even feel the cold anymore!

Shouldering their guns, they follow their commands. Left Shoulder! Right Shoulder! And then the command FIRE! Boom! Boom! The sounds of my two- gun salute crashes in my ears and then, in this unimaginable moment, the sun slides behind the clouds and my gaze slips away. I am carried back, way back, into the pages of my history, back to where my 200 parks in four years adventure first began. Back and back I go into the giggles of a nine-year-old little girl, making faces at the world passing her by. Come with me on my Two Hundred National Park Friendship Tour! It is an adventure that you will never forget! It's going to be good! Scratch that! It is going to be great!

Come with me! I wouldn't think of going without you!

Your New Friend,
Aida

The Way You Hit Home Runs In Life
Is To Always Know You Did Your
Absolute Best!

Aida Frey

FIELD OF DREAMS

Dyersville, Iowa

Hey Everybody!

How's it going? Care to take a ride back into my nine-year-old life with me? Let's go!

My parents 2004 white Chevy Impala trucks along under the early afternoon sky! It does really good in a well-marked yellow and white lined grocery store asphalt parking lot and on America's busy and open highways. Holding its hood up high amongst its fellow SUVs, crossovers, hatchbacks, mini-vans and hybrids, it is our mode of transportation as we become a traditional part of the country's highway landscape and has been an old faithful friend taking me into my Two Hundred National Park Friendship Tour!

Yes! Our car is like an old friend. I guess that's why I named it Friendship. Always on time, loyal, a great listener and the most sincere piece of metal on this earth, Friendship is a family friend and someone that we know we can count on! Zigzagging around hillsides, clinging to dirt roads, it drives through falling leaves, snow storms and out-of-nowhere downpours and puts up with my dad's jokes! Yes! It's a great sport. It hails all the new places we pull into and seems to gives us an always approving nod as it clambers down old hillsides, braces itself for the spirit of the road and takes us carefully over spots blocked with the undergrowth of time.

Sometimes I feel like I am riding shotgun and my family and I are reclaiming America's frontier when we take to the road. Far from any city-centers, I feel as if I am lounging in the wonderful feelings of adventure and freedom! I can still hear the beeping of car horns my nine- year-old ears took on as we took to the highway on our way from Chicago to Iowa. I remember it was like a makeshift parking lot as we disappeared into the line of traffic stitching the highway.

I consider myself a futuristic kid with always an eye on tomorrow. Pretty interesting coming from a kid who loves the past and history! Even back then I remember thinking we should flatten the highways and build one gigantic bicycle lane! Funny how no one shouts out stuff like this! Riding around in the backseat you think of all sorts of stuff! Kids can think, can't they?!

The great thing about being the only kid in the car on a road trip is I have the whole backseat to myself, windows and all! My little girl nose presses against the car window, watching the world fly by. Goodbye clouds in the sky! Do you know I am up to something?! I think you do! I am giggling so much I drop to the backseat and then roll over onto the floor of the car!

My parents have no clue as to what is going on! They cannot figure out why I am laughing so much. Cars on I80 are honking their horns at us and you can see people in the passing cars laughing, pointing and waving! They are tooting their horns at our car and pointing to me in the backseat and smiling and laughing! I am laughing so hard! My parents still don't have a clue as to what is going on! I can't stop giggling. Too bad my parents don't have a convertible. This would be even more fun if the top was down!

This is one of those not-so-long drives but long enough for me to laugh myself silly! We are on our way from Chicago to the corn field in Iowa that was The Field of Dreams baseball field that was made into a baseball diamond for the movie Field of Dreams with Kevin Costner. Yes! It does really exist! And we are headed there right now, but for the moment I am having a great time making my own fun being a nine-year-old playing in the window of my parent's car.

My little girl nose presses against the window of the car as if it is in the bloom of a flower. Speckled with sun, my face is glowing. The clouds move over the sun stealing it away from the car window and I turn and rest my back against the back door. We are just a few miles away from the corn field where the movie Field of Dreams was filmed.

We are going to play baseball on the baseball diamond they built in the cornfield for the movie. It will be fun, but I am having so much fun right now!

Stripes of sun are dancing on the car window again and I turn and press my face against the window of the car again this time as if it is my pillow. People in passing cars are waving to me and grinning and they are honking their horn at my fanged smile! My mother glances over at me with a suspicious grin, she may be onto something. We are off of I-80 and continue driving down the road. I cannot stop laughing and topple back on the floor of the car. My mom wants to know what is so funny. There is a look on my face that she just can't figure out and of course I have my hands cupped over my mouth. Do I dare smile? I do! So, I look at my mom and then I take away my hands and the tiniest of smiles cross my lips and then I break out into this humongous grin and my mom sees my fake fangs and she starts laughing! Yes my friends! I am wearing vampire teeth and scaring the freeway with fun!

We pull into the Field of Dreams parking lot and my dad parks. He turns around and looks at me and he starts cracking up. And now he is on to my secret! He now knows why people were honking at us! I was making vampire faces at the cars on the highway from Chicago to Iowa! My parents and I were laughing so much! I took the vampire fangs out of my mouth and then my mom put them away in the glove compartment. Laughing, we get out of the car to see the famous cornfield that became a famous baseball diamond! And there it is before us, just like in the movie! WOW! I can't believe that I am seeing this! You see, you get used to seeing something on a movie screen or on television, but when you are actually there and it is there, you just can't believe it all! It is just amazing!

I am so glad to get out of the car and stretch my legs in the Field of Dreams cornfield. I feel happy! My dad adjusts his baseball cap and shouts, "Play ball!" We run to the field still laughing about my fanged face in the car window just a few hours ago! I loved the movie Field of Dreams so to actually run across the famous cornfield that was turned into a baseball field for the movie is really a cartwheel moment for me. My dad thinks of everything! He brought mitts, baseballs, baseball bats and baseball hats. And there I am stealing bases on a cornfield!

The play-by-play sports broadcaster (in my mind) is broadcasting all over the world how Aida Frey is stealing bases and hitting homers and making baseball history! The crowd is taking pictures of me with their cell phones! It is the first ever baseball game played in a cornfield and the crowd is going crazy! The crowd is eating peanuts and hotdogs with their own personally inspired toppings! It is a great day in baseball as Aida Frey masters the ultimate weapon of baseball and slides again into home plate! She's safe and the crowd goes nuts! And it is another great day in baseball, in Iowa, and in the cornfield of the movie The Field of Dreams!

I hope you had a blast! I had a great time!

Your Friend Always,
Aida

P.S. I hear my dad talking about Effigy Mounds National Monument and that means we are probably going to be headed there after Field of Dreams. I can hardly wait! You see, we just pick up and do things on the spur of the moment when we are travelling. We don't have to check flight or train schedules. We just hit the road and look forward to our next exciting adventure! Good-bye Field of Dreams! Effigy Mounds, here we come!

P.P.S Before we get to Effigy Mounds National Monument in Iowa, I would like to talk about my good friend, Tom.

There Is Something Special
About My Friend Tom.
He Is Stuffed
With Love~

Aida Frey

TOM

Hey Everybody!

May I introduce to you my dear friend Tom?

In the rustle of the cornfield was Tom. When I was tossing the baseball, there was Tom. Yep! You guessed it! Tom was in my knapsack, in the backseat, when I was making fanged faces on I80 all the way from Chicago to Iowa! Tom went with me when I first began going to America's national parks. Forgive me for being a bit over-sentimental about Tom. Tom remains one of those small things in life that are very big deals and his age even now remains unknown.

A long time ago, I played with him online. He was code 30. He was a fox and I don't know why he was my favorite. There were certainly more gorgeous than Tom. There was the stuffed monkey with the little ballet slippers and the octopus with the top hat and then there was the adorable toothpick black bear. Yes! There were certainly more out there that were cuter than Tom, but none of them more huggable and lovable than him.

Tom was not only a great friend, but he was just good at putting up with it all. He wore hand-me-downs from my other stuffed animals. Tom had a ranger hat, a baseball uniform, jeans and a cape. Tom was well-travelled. He has been all over. He went with me locally on Halloween. He dressed as a ghost! We went all over the neighborhood trick-or-treating. He actually made a pretty good haul on candy as I remember. He went to the movies with me and of course to America's National Parks. He even had his own national parks passport! I filled it out for him! Tom and I were hiking buddies. He used to go in my back pack.

Naturally, Tom was included in all our family functions. Anytime, any relatives came to town or we went visiting, Tom went too. He had his own suitcase and really was the life of the party. He was nicknamed Tom French Frey! Good thing he had a sense of humor. Of course, Tom is retired now, but I must admit he knew my childhood well. He was a big part of it and my trusted friend and confidant! Today, he sits comfortably on a shelf in my room with an eye on my cute little pink polar bear.

Your Friend Always,
Aida

Every stuffed animal
Should have a kid like
Aida to cuddle.

Tom

Hello!

I am Tom. I am Code 30.

I wanted to sneak into Aida's pages before she starts talking about our trip to Effigy Mounds. It was a great trip! I hope she tells you about how we jumped in the big leaf beds there! It was a blast! I could go on and on, but I will let her tell you about it. After all, it is her life biography, but one of these days, do not be too surprised if I come out with my biography too! Can you imagine a biography about a stuffed fox? Hey! I'm pretty interesting!

I was born a stuffed toy animal, a darn cute one too! I am a white-chested red fox full of charisma! Now of course I have floppy legs and I am sure that I have some fancy stuffing but I am really quite simple. I am not glamorized by locks of satin hair and a tummy sparkling of sequins like some of my buddies. I was just born a soft simple stuffed little toy red fox that came to life in the Frey family. By the way, my middle name is Frenchie. Tom French Frey! Get it?! Remember, having a sense of humor is very important in life! It is the key to being happy!

At times prankish, funny and a jokester, I was always well-behaved, friendly and filled with silliness. I am, and will always be, Aida's admiring audience. And, in many ways, I have signaled my importance in the Frey family. Take the time the Freys forgot me in a hotel room. Can you imagine? It was on one of their trips to the national parks and I was left sitting on the hotel bed alone in a strange city! My heart sank when I was left in that hotel room, let me tell you. It is all coming back to me now.

Aida and her parents were on their way to Chattanooga, Tennessee when they realized I wasn't in the backseat. Filled with panic, they turned the car around (as the story goes) and raced like crazy back to get me and there I was, faithful Tom, waiting for them, as usual. They all hugged me like crazy when they found me. I was just sitting on the hotel bed where they left me. What could I do? They took the car! Soon as we got home they threw me in the washing machine. Some welcome home party. Hey, you can't figure everyone out! I just learned in life you just have to roll with it!

But really, The Freys are great! And I have really had a blast with them! I have known Aida since she was a little kid and have visited America's beautiful national parks. We have hiked together, seen wild animals, taken in the beauty of nature and together have been an imaginative resource for each other! Aida imagines a lot with me and I imagine a lot with her! Aida is right! I even have a national parks passport! It makes me smile that she loved me enough to want me to have a passport!

I often wonder how stuffed animals shape communities and the world. I have heard Aida say many times that she never knew why I was her favorite or even where my name came from. But she has been a great friend to me. I mean it is not your everyday stuffed toy fox that has a ranger hat! So what that I have hand-me-downs from other stuffed animals? I know Aida loves me! It is not every day that a stuffed toy animal can see America's national parks and other cool stuff in a kid's backpack!

I love you Aida! So glad I could be part of your childhood and be part of your pages. Forgive me for sneaking into your book! I just couldn't resist! Look me up once in a while when you have time! I am on the second shelf of your closet. Maybe we can see a One Direction concert sometime! They are my favorite group too! And of course, I'm always up for visiting America's national parks! And you are right Aida, I do have my eye on that cute pink polar bear of yours!

Your Old Friend,
Tom

P.S. Oh! One more thing, Aida, thanks for making me feel real.

Sometimes
All a kid needs
Is a bed of leaves~

Aida Frey

EFFIGY MOUNDS NATIONAL MONUMENT

Harpers Ferry, Iowa

Hey Everybody!

Leaving The Field of Dreams baseball field didn't work for me. It was too soon! I liked this place so much because it was just so simple and it felt so easy being there! I just didn't want to leave although we were there for a long time! I could have stayed there much longer throwing that baseball of ours! Hey! I was just warming up there in that cornfield! Had we stayed there longer, I think I could have been a great pitcher and also stolen tons of bases! But my dad wanted to show us Effigy Mounds which was not too far. So I hopped back in the ol' Impala and after waving goodbye to Iowa's Field of Dreams, my dad stepped on the gas and we were on the road to our next adventure!

Now, I want to tell you something. Trying to get from the Field of Dreams baseball field to Effigy Mounds was no easy thing. I remember we had zigzagged our way for what felt like quite some time. We are trying to follow this huge map that my mom was trying to make sense of. The map was so enormous it almost filled up the whole front seat. I remember munching on this yummy turkey and cheese sandwich in the backseat and licking mustard off my fingers as we drove through these beautiful farmlands and back roads. It was all great until the road got rough. The back roads were very bumpy as we went up and down on them. My parents' car wasn't taking too kindly to the bumps and neither was Tom. I wasn't either for that matter. I remember grabbing Tom and getting mustard all over him. Tom was a trooper and I hung on to him for dear life. Leaning into the front seat of my chauffeured

Impala, I told my parents I longed for a cold drink. I was ready to get out of the car and I was trying to be nice about it!

My mother tried to comfort me by trying to convince me that our bumpy road was behind us when I let out a squeal. We were approaching a sign that clearly said we were entering Effigy Mounds. Well, I didn't know that my parents could cheer so loud! They were like a bunch of kids! The three of us started clapping! The Impala became a car of super huge grins! Slowly we drove by the sign that welcomed us to Effigy Mounds. My dad took a picture of it. I think he couldn't believe we were off of that bumpy two-lane road. I will tell you the truth, I couldn't believe it either!

I couldn't wait for my dad to stop the car! You have to remember, I was just a nine-year- old and I had been in the car way too long! My dad parked and we all grabbed our bottles of water and I grabbed Tom and put him in the back of my knapsack. We were ready to hit the hiking trails. We had been told that Effigy Mounds was known for its picturesque footpaths and I just couldn't wait to take to the trails!

It was hot and humid as we got out of the car. I recall the heat greeting us like we were celebrities! Embracing us, it almost knocked us over! It felt like it was asking us for our autograph! It even tickled my ears when I took a breath! You know, we live in a word world. But there are really no fancy words for weather on a hot day. But there are no fancy words to describe a hot and humid day. It was just hot and muggy. So, I took a swig of water and Tom and I set out as adventurers to see Effigy Mounds and, of course, to tackle the remainder of the sizzling day.

A rough dirt trail is before us. Effigy Mounds is the first national park that I have ever visited and I remember I was so very excited. And I must admit, I was also excited about having an excuse to get muddy! Huffing and puffing, Tom and I made great hiking partners! Although looking back on it, it does seem like I did most of the work! I remember myself running through this newly discovered leaf-rustling and orchid-blooming world. Even as a kid of nine, I was fascinated by beautiful places and I still am. Effigy Mounds was beautiful and I loved throwing the leaves up in the air and crunching them under my feet. It was the first time I had ever been in a national park and I was the happiest kid on earth!

I remember seeing birds perching in the shade and I was just captivated by the beauty of it. I was astonished by the prettiness that was surrounding me and the bigness of the park. It was huge! But it was in this hike with my parents, the first hike of my life, that I made my first connection with nature. I couldn't believe all of the different footpaths along the way and the heaps of leaves that I thought were bigger than I was and the fun of just playing in nature and being a kid! It was here in the leaves that I experienced my country in a natural sort of way without cars and beeping horns and bulldozers. I remember leaves falling aimlessly from the trees and I wondered what would happen if a leaf got stuck in the wind. How would I rescue it?

It took about twenty minutes to make it up the hiking trail. I remember it being totally awesome! I was a little girl hiding behind trees, my feet crunching the leaves. It felt really good for me to make it to the top and see the mounds outlined in white. My family and I stood there looking at the shape of the mounds. It was so amazing for me to see. What was really amazing to learn was that the Native Americans, a zillion years ago, created the mounds mostly in bears, lizards, turtles and birds! But they are in different sizes and shapes and they have a mystery about them like you've never seen. I think they hold the mystery of the earth! They have secrets! As a nine-year-old at the time, I probably didn't absorb it all. But I do now. History is just really something. I remember finding it fascinating the way the mounds just rise out of the ground and have lasted so long. It was really something to see and my eyes were wide with amazement. But it was the leaves I want to talk about.

Naturally occurring leaf piles formed by the wind decorate the zigzagging footpaths. The leaves, as they fall from the trees, each leaf falling comes with a hypnotic story of its own. I kind of feel that when the leaves fall and drop on the grass, they are really giving the grass a hug! I think leaves speak such a simple language of freedom. The ground, piled high with leaves, is just so beautiful. Trust me! There is nothing prettier than leaf beds. Don't be so quick to rake the leaves either. They benefit wildlife and suppress weeds in your garden!

First of all, it was like the grass was waving at you when you walked through it. Its bellies flatten as you stepped on it but then it came right back up, the blades of grass welcoming your every step! Nature has its own welcome mat, you know? I remember the grass stood close to me and it felt so wonderful to be in its beauty. It felt so calm and soothing. It was just so pretty.

We came down the trail and coming down was a lot easier than going up. I was all excited. I remember thinking that the trail was just as pretty when you are coming down as it was when you were going up. Somehow though, the trees and light looked different. I don't know. I can't really explain it. Maybe it has something to do with being a nine-year-old and waving to the sinking sun. Then again, maybe Tom has all of the answers!

One more thing that I wanted to mention about this trip to Effigy Mounds and that was what happened after the hike. The sun was disappearing into the sky. The air was very still. It was as if Effigy Mounds did not want us to say goodbye yet. My dad wanted us to get to the Visitors' Bureau. I remember it as if it were yesterday. There were two ladies behind the counter and they were getting ready to close. But they stayed open and started talking to us all about The Junior Ranger Program. Immediately I wanted to do it! As a Junior Ranger you get patches and badges and pins from the national parks you visit. You get a passport book that is stamped every time you visit a park and you make a promise to learn about the parks and tell your Ranger story.

I am very proud of my visit to Effigy Mounds. I think maybe firsts in life are a big deal. I mean like you probably always will remember your first day in kindergarten or your first day in high school. This is how I feel about my visit to Effigy Mounds. Visiting Effigy Mounds was like peeking into a beautiful natural wonderland. I learned so much! I saw so much! I saw things that I never even knew existed such as the mounds. I am so amazed that these mounds are here today after all of the centuries that have gone by. What an amazing feeling! So! Welcome to my Junior Ranger story! Welcome to America Can I Have Your Autograph, The Story of Junior Ranger Aida Frey!

The white glow of the oncoming car headlights wash over us as we head back to Chicago. The day has long since gone. Cars speed by us on the highway. The black nighttime sky seems to turn the headlights of all the passing cars into ghosts. Too bad it is so dark outside. I giggle.

No one can see that I put my vampire teeth back in my mouth. I smile a fanged smile.

I am nine-year-old Aida Frey, child car jokester. I give a final bow to the moon glistening upon my highway audience. Closing my eyes, I send one last giggle off into the night. What a fun day!

Your Friend Always,
Aida

Nothing beats being a kid!

Aida Frey

THE MARK TWAIN BOYHOOD HOME & MUSEUM

Hannibal, Missouri

Hey Everybody!

The Mark Twain Home Foundation has a goal. It is to get the word out on Mark Twain (Samuel Clemens became Mark Twain) and his works and show the reason behind his stories for kids and grownups alike all over the world. Mark Twain's boyhood home is a designated National Historic Landmark! Come on! Let's check it out! Samuel Clemens whose pen name was Mark Twain was known all over the world. He was a famous writer. I love his writing. I love his stories. I love the way he uses his childhood escapades and picks his boyhood home Hannibal, Missouri to set the adventures of Tom Sawyer, Huck Finn and Becky Thatcher. Hannibal, Missouri has definitely become a magical historical spot because of his writing. What is even more, his childhood experiences have made Hannibal famous!

My parents and I went to Hannibal, Missouri where the Tom Sawyer house was. The stifling hot and humid weather hit me the moment I stepped out of the car. I remember just feeling zapped of energy. I must admit, for a moment, I didn't want to venture out into the humidity. My energy came back when I saw the amazing old-fashioned buildings and cobblestone streets that took us back to when Mark Twain was a kid! We saw kids and adults dressed like Huck Finn, Becky Thatcher and Tom Sawyer. It was amazing. You just felt like you had entered into another world. They gave a presentation and then took us into Mark Twain's house back into the 1800s on Cardiff Hill. You felt as if you had just entered into their adventures.

The Mississippi River was right there and you could look out and see the old paddlewheels. Up and down the river you saw small islands and it reminded me of how in the story Huck and Tom paddled over to the islands and the town panicked because they were missing but in reality they had dozed off on one of the islands! The islands bring the characters in the book to life, as does his cave outside of town which we drove to and which I was afraid to go in. A side note, I eventually grew out of my fear of caves but would have liked if I hadn't had my fear then. Who knows all of the discoveries I could have made!

What made me really feel like I was so part of the story was painting the fence! Oh wow! Tom was told by his aunt to whitewash this fence and he didn't want to do it. So he got a whole bunch of kids to come and he kicked back in the cool grass while all these kids painted the fence. Well, I painted some of the fence while I was there and it was so awesome. I felt as if I just jumped in the pages. It was such an incredible feeling! It was a great experience for me as a kid to feel like I was one of the kids in Mark Twain's pages! Talk about doing something different! This is why I urge everyone to get off of the couch, disconnect from the Internet and get out there and see the amazing things that are in America! America is so much fun!

You see, I picked up a paintbrush and started painting a little bit of the fence and I felt like I was doing something in the story that really made the story work! The paint brush for me was like a magic wand and it was as if Tom Sawyer, Becky Thatcher and Huck Finn were right next to me! I discovered a bit of myself in the story. I was part of the activity. It was as if I was one of his friends! Painting the fence made me feel like I was doing something that helped create the heart of the story! I felt like I was one of the friends painting the fence while Tom was on the cool grass napping away.

I want to say something very interesting here. Get into his mind set and you start to know what he was thinking and being accustomed to his thoughts and how his character shaped the tale of the story. I think as a kid you should be able to experience your imagination. Imagination helps you experience new things! I loved painting this fence. It has been a highlight in my life as a kid!

Thank you Hannibal, Missouri! You've got the formula for making a kid feel great and for bringing Tom Sawyer, Becky Thatcher and Huck Finn to life! Thank you for making me feel like Huck and Tom and Becky are my friends! It was a great day in Hannibal! Yes! It was a wonderful day!

I hope everyone enjoyed Hannibal!

Your Friend Always,
Aida

It's OK to be afraid.
I think being afraid
Is what makes you brave!

Aida Frey

THE SCAREDY-CAT

Hey Everybody!

We all have our favorites, but I want to tell you one of my favorite authors of all time! I admired Samuel Langhorne Clemens, also known as Mark Twain. Mark Twain was his pen name. He was a very famous writer from Missouri. He was a prankster and he made his small boyhood town, Hannibal, Missouri very famous. I admired his barefoot days on the river. It was all about blue skies and the river keeping his imagination alive! He also had a love and fascination for caves which I acquired after we left Hannibal! Can you imagine!

I want to share some interesting things about Samuel Clemens. He was many things. He was a business man and a family man. He was a typesetter, a river pilot, an author and a speaker. He was an American humorist but he had a very serious side. He was very dedicated to dealing with the issues of class-differences, poverty and slavery. He travelled the world. One thing that I found very interesting about him was that he was born during Halley's Comet and died when the comet returned 74 years later! Wow!

It seems as if Samuel Clemens wasn't afraid of anything. He was a fun-loving kid who was very mischievous. He carried out many adventures that you don't understand until you start to do some of the things that he did (such as painting the fence which I already talked about a little earlier). He was all about enjoying himself and having a great time in his kid life! I feel kind of bad that I did not explore the cave when I was there in his boyhood home town, but I had a fear of caves at the time. But soon, as you keep reading, you will see how I became a cave lover. I really think a lot of my change of heart and mind was due to the fact that I didn't go into the cave when I was visiting Samuel Clemens' boyhood town and I really regretted not doing so. I don't want to miss out on anything as a kid in life. There are so many good things out there to experience.

It is clear that Samuel Clemens never grew tired of his treasure-digging adventures. But the one thing that really stuck out with Samuel Clemens was his love for caves. The cave was definitely a big joy in his life. The caves took him deep down into the secret passages of the earth. It took him even below the river which was a huge love for him. He was willing to stop fishing to go cave exploring and carry out his adventures. He never lost his fascination of caves.

I think he was afraid of thunderstorms. Actually it was the lightning that made the child in him afraid. So remember, it is not just you that is afraid of things or me. Everyone has a little child in them at some point in life that comes out. It may come out many times for no reason. Fear is not something that we can easily figure out.

We don't always understand why we are afraid of something. I think I grew out of my fear of caves, but I don't really know. You always have to be careful and think things through, but sometimes you just have to ignore your fears and remember Mark Twain's carefree barefoot days on the river! Funny how a girl from Chicago grew to share a famous writer's love and fascination for caves! Yes! Life is really funny sometimes!

Your Friend Always,
Aida

Friendship
Is sharing a bottle of pop
With someone special~

Aida Frey

FRIENDSHIP

Hey Everybody!

I once had a dream about a kid dusting off a canoe and we both got into the canoe and paddled away. We laughed all day and then we paddled back to shore with the fading sun behind us. It was a great friendship day. I awoke giggling! Of course it was just a dream but it made me realize that friendship is magic. Friendships can involve a walk in the snow, giggles at school or congratulating a classmate for making great grades! Homework friendship is when you share your smarts with a classmate, acquire wisdom and make amazing homework discoveries! Friendship is so many things. Friendship is the tapping of rain on the kitchen window. Friendship is the black swivel chair that I spin on when I'm on the phone! Friendship is my parents' 2004 white Chevy Impala that takes us on our national park trips and to the cool stuff we see along the way!

My suitcase sits by the front door in my house. It is so funny but everything that I take with me is all assembled in like little heaps in the hallway. Just before we go on one of our vacations my suitcase is checked and rechecked by my mom just to make sure that I don't forget anything. We have a buddy system. I let her know what I want to bring and I pack it. She goes through my suitcase and makes sure I didn't forget anything that she wants me to bring! My mom is a good friend. We like a lot of the same things and we seem to always be filled with the same anticipation and excitement! Although, I must admit that I do seem to get more excited about playing hockey and watching it on television than she does.

The street hisses with cars. It looks like the cars are crawling around in this white maze. Huffing and puffing, the road tries to support all the weighty baggage on top of it. After all, everyone knows Chicago suffers from bad cases of city snow. Have I mentioned to you that I am from the windy city of Chicago?! Yep! Chicago is my hometown. It is like an old friend to me, really! It is always there when I go to bed at night and it is there outside my window to greet me when I get up in the morning. Sometimes I look outside at night before I go to bed and I think Chicago leads straight up to the moon! You wait, one day the wind will blow in a certain way and Chicago will be on the moon!

Sometimes I think friendship is being by yourself and just enjoying your favorite spot! Maybe watching frogs in a pond or watching your favorite television show or riding your bike or maybe just doing nothing at all. I think everyone enjoys the roar of approval, but it is nice to just be alone, like what you are doing and enjoy some daily thinking on your own! I think the key to friendship is to always be real and to always remember everyone has star qualities. Everyone has their own buddy nature. I think one thing that really makes a good friend is if someone is a good listener! Some kids are great at talking and some kids are great at listening. Some kids are really compassionate and just make you feel great because they are around.

So, I must listen to myself right now and climb into bed! Night is falling and too soon the alarm clock is going to be shrieking at me. In the morning I will awaken in the arms of my alarm clock. My dad wants to get an early start. Tomorrow we are going to the Sears Tower! I am very excited. Of course it is in Chicago so we are close but we like to get an early start. It is funny, but I know that I will be throwing my pillow at that alarm clock in the morning! I am not sure if friendship is an alarm clock by the way!!

See you in the morning! Remember, we are off to The Sears Tower and a wonderful time! Oh yes! One more thing! Set your alarm clocks so you are ready to leave with us! Can't wait!

Your Friend Always,
Aida

I am on top of the world!
Look at me!
I am playing hide and
seek with the sky!

Aida Frey

THE SEARS TOWER/THE WILLIS TOWER

Chicago, Illinois

Hey Everybody!

Your ears pop when you go up the high-speed elevator ride to the 103rd floor of The Sears Tower (Willis Tower) in Chicago. It is this 103rd floor that makes you feel as if you are standing on top of the world! Oh wow! I could hardly catch my breath as the elevator doors opened and I edged my way out among the crowd. I looked through the wall of windows and discovered a life-altering secret! Pssssst ... want to hear it?? A clownish moon ducks behind the Sears Tower at night and shines on Chicago and its excitement tickles the city!

The Sears Tower is the first stop on my America Can I Have Your Autograph tour! Standing on the 103rd floor, I feel like I can jump through the clouds and hold the sun in my hands! The view really puts your mind somewhere else! It is utterly thrilling! Standing in America's tallest building (which is not just a tourist attraction and cultural landmark but is home to bunches and bunches of companies), I feel like my dad just bought me a ticket to the sky!

I would like to stop here and invite my dad into my pages. He has a really cool story to tell about The Sears Tower. So, I will be back in a few minutes after he's done. I think you'll like my dad and find him very interesting. By the way his name is Shawn. Oh! My mom's name is Norma. All my trips are a family thing. We have a blast when we go on vacation! Ok! Here is my Dad. "Hello! I'm Shawn, Aida's Dad. And I just want to say that when I was about ten years old, my parents got divorced and my mom put our house up for sale. We lived in Chicago and they were just starting to build The Sears Tower downtown. Interesting, one of the engineers who built the sky scraper bought my parent's house (Aida's grandparents' house). It kind of makes me happy to think that one of the major engineers who worked on this iconic sky scraper may have had breakfast in our kitchen where I had breakfast before he left for work to work on the tower! The thought of it has me borrowing some of my daughter Aida's butterflies! Okay everyone and now it is back to Aida. By the way, nice to meet everyone! We are having a great time! Norma, Aida's mom, says hi! And we are so happy that you could come along with us for Aida's 200 National Park tour!"

I am back! My parents are great by the way. They are basically pretty cool people! Okay! Back to the Sears Tower which is now called the Willis Tower. I just refer to it as The Sears Tower because I grew up with it with that name! Okay, so the Sears Tower is blasted with sunlight! Oh wow! I mean, you get out of that long elevator ride and the bright lights are turned on! Yes! Sunlight pours in through the windows and you want to tell the sun to go back to bed! But everyone loves it and everyone is at the windows. The huge wall of windows is just thrilling! It is like you are out in the cosmos and you can knock on the Heavens! The closer you get to the windows, you see tops of buildings and the streets below are filled with little tiny matchbox cars and there are ants all over the streets! What I mean is you are so high up that the people down below look like little ants! You can see Lake Michigan and the steel mills in Gary, Indiana. (We will be going there soon by the way)! It is all so exciting! But you cannot be afraid of heights and give yourself courage! Now of course I think everyone gets a little scared when they are up so high, but just don't think about it. Just focus on the moment and what you are seeing and don't let your mind go out of the moment. I think being afraid of heights is like being afraid of thunderstorms.

I want to share something here. If you are a bit scared of heights, The Sears Tower is definitely high up. What I suggest is you just think that you are dancing on the beams of the sky! Just become a cloud-walker! Concentrate on what makes you laugh and just fill your mind up with good thoughts and run the fear out of your head! Once the fear is gone, you will be a happy kid!

Ok! Now the greatest thrill ever! My ledge experience! The sky is illuminated with light as you step into this area encased in glass. There is no floor! Can you believe it?! You are really standing on glass and it is like nothing is holding you up. The floor out on the ledge is all clear like you are standing on air! So the sunlight is slashing the clouds and I feel as if I have been dipped in the sun! I am sheer as glass! Nothing is below me, I am standing on air! Look at me! I am an astronaut. I am weightless. I am looking into the face of the sun! I am looking at the tops of the trees! I am in this glistening, fascinating orbit like nothing that I have ever experienced. I know that as I stand here I will never forget my experience of playing hide and seek with the sky and for feeling like I am on top of the world!

And so as we wait for the elevator to come and get us, a playful smile falls across my face. I have had such a fun time today! I am going to really sleep well tonight. You know, if you have a great day, you sleep better at night! Sears Tower, I want to tell you something. I heard a secret about you. I heard you pull the covers off of the city during the day and tuck the city in with stars at night! Thank you Chicago! Thank you for the Sears Tower. And may I say Chicago, you look fabulous!

Your Friend Always,
Aida

When I go on a trip to
America's national parks
My suitcase is packed with joy!

Aida Frey

THE JOHN DILLINGER MUSEUM

Hammond, Indiana

Hey Everybody!

Remember I told you about my suitcase by the front door? Well, my mom snapped the handle into place and my dad tossed it in the trunk of our Impala. Yes! I slid into the backseat quite a bit ago and I can feel my suitcase knocking around in the trunk. We should be in Indiana very soon and I am so thrilled! I mean who wouldn't be! We are off to the John Dillinger Museum in Crown Point, Indiana! How cool is that! My goodness, I am going to an outlaw's museum!

Imagine visiting a famous outlaw! Well, that's just what we are about to do! Well, almost! There is much legend surrounding my next stop! I mean can you imagine an outlaw having his own museum? I have heard that visiting this museum is an adventure! It teaches you about crime and about how the FBI worked so hard to control this period of time and make people feel safe. But it was an interesting period of time for America.

We arrived at this famous place and not a moment too soon. Sometimes, I get very antsy in the backseat but it is mostly because I am so excited about reaching our destination. My face is pressed to the backseat glass window. My eyes are squinting as I am looking for this famous outlaw's museum. My dad gives the official, "We are here," and parks the car. I am thrilled and unhook my seatbelt and pop the door open. Stepping out of the car, I wave to my mom and yell out, "Come on! Let's go!" I get impatient when I know a great time is waiting for me! I just can't wait to see cool stuff!

From the second we walked into the John Dillinger Museum, I was intrigued with what appears to be the artifacts left from his crimes. I saw the trousers that he wore when he got shot. What I found very interesting about The John Dillinger Museum was the way that I felt when I walked in. I felt like I actually knew John Dillinger. I know it sounds crazy, but I actually felt like I had met him before. It is as if you were transported backwards in time. I don't know. The stories that we were told about him just seemed so unimaginable. I mean you just cannot believe what you are hearing. Let me tell you some stuff.

One story really stands out to me about one of America's most famous outlaws and it is the story of the wooden gun. I would like to tell this story because it just filled up my mind so much I couldn't think about anything else for days! John Dillinger was an outlaw but he taught the world not to underestimate the criminal mind, especially his criminal mind! He had quite an imagination. I am not kidding. He transformed his prison cell and the fix he was in by using his creativity. He bluffed the prison guards with a piece of wood. You see, he made them think it was a gun! Can you imagine that?! The prison guards really thought what he had in his hand was a gun, but it wasn't! That was the amazing trick. I am even more amazed as I talk about it!

One after the other, after the other, John Dillinger bluffed Crown Point Jailhouse officials into captivity, driven by this false fear of being killed. He didn't even have a gun! It was a piece of wood but he tricked them! He tricked them with his smarts! Then John Dillinger, still remaining calm, took the only master set of keys the jail had and he left. To add to Sheriff Holley's further embarrassment, Dillinger stole her own personal police car for his artful escape! Oh wow! Can you imagine?!

Well, as the story goes, the Crown Point jailhouse was in an uproar! It was absolute chaos! Everyone was ratting on everyone! Everyone was accusing everyone for being responsible for the escape! But I really do think that it was Dillinger's creation of story, his flash of storytelling smarts and his wisdom that caught the guards off guard at the jailhouse that was so impressive. The guards did not give Dillinger enough credit! They did not think that he was that crafty. Clearly, they underestimated him and the look-alike wooden gun was like a powerful tornado that just ripped through the jailhouse! Like crumbling brick, the jailhouse was really hopelessly buried in Dillinger's creative caper. Although the accusations began to fly in a human tornado among the prison guards and jailhouse personnel, no one could deny that this creative human hurricane of the 1920s and 30s, John Dillinger, outsmarted them all, one-by-one!

As the story goes, after John Dillinger's famous escape, officials had found an old washboard under the bed of his prison cell. This washboard was believed to be a prop left to try to create a scene and make prison officials think that it was whittled from the missing top brace of the washboard. This was all staged by Dillinger, himself, to protect those who helped him escape. Wow! I just find this so amazing!

There is no real proof that a real gun was ever smuggled into the jail and given to Dillinger and no such gun has ever been found, but interestingly enough, the wooden gun did surface and is at the John Dillinger Museum and I SAW IT!! I have to say that to hear the story and then see it just makes you feel like you stepped into history and like you were really there in that jailhouse when Dillinger bluffed his way out. I just sat and pictured the situation in my mind and find it very interesting how he displayed his "smarts" and remained so calm with his plan to gain his freedom. Dillinger's fake gun plan worked and for a period in history, Crown Point Jailhouse was behind its own bars!!

Indiana's first female sheriff, Sheriff Lillian Holley, who was as I have already mentioned tricked by Dillinger's fake wooden gun trick and had her own personal police car used in the escape, died in 1994 at the age of 103 years old. Sheriff Holley was well loved by her town! Wow! Can you imagine that she was 103 years old?! What an experience to live with!

I can only say that this is some story and this is some adventure for me, just a kid from Chicago! Leaving the John Dillinger Museum I know that crime does not pay but I also cannot help but be completely taken in by Dillinger's wooden gun story and this part of history! Wow! What a day! Thank you Indiana! Thank you for The John Dillinger Museum! What a story!

Oh! One more thing everyone! Just when we were leaving The John Dillinger Museum, my dad learned that Jean Shepherd's boyhood house was not far. Jean Shepherd, author of A Christmas Story, wrote one of my favorite movies of all time! So! Come along with us everyone! We are headed there now. You are all invited! Fasten your seatbelts! We are on our way to the Christmas Story House from A Christmas Story movie! I've got a feeling this is going to be another fun adventure!

Your Friend Always,
Aida

JEAN SHEPHERD'S BOYHOOD HOME

(The Author of a Christmas Story)
Hammond, Indiana

Hey Everybody!

Do you want to know what my family and I said when we heard that Christmas Story author Jean Shepherd's boyhood town is only three miles from The John Dillinger Museum? I'll tell you what we said! "GIVE US THE MAP! We are there!"

You see, we love cool stuff! We will drive hours out of our way to visit someplace that has a story to it. We travel the roads that have been around for decades and decades. Something looks like it is interesting and we are there! You see, you have just caught us at something we are good at, seeing the cool stuff America is made of!

Hopping back on the highway we head for Jean Shepherd's childhood home. We have just left the amazing John Dillinger Museum. I am still remembering the museum with so much excitement! Three miles down the road, closely following the map, we are like three reporters hot on the trail to find this famous author's boyhood home and learn of his story! A drop of my soda spills from my cup as my dad makes a turn off of the highway. My eyes follow its slow disappearance on the seat as I wipe it up. I take a deep breath. Chicago has been left behind a long time ago.

Twisting and turning down streets that may have composed the author's growing up experiences, I am filled with anticipation. The inside of our car is filled with rounds and rounds of excitement. Jean

Shepherd had a nickname of Shep! He was a storyteller and of course a great novelist. Sitting in the backseat, I am chuckling quietly along with this great author and his adventures with his story character Ralphie. Jean Shepherd's A Christmas Story was written in such a friendly style. Jean Shepherd does such a great job in taking his readers into his smattering of stories. I begin to wonder if he walked to school on the streets I am seeing, if he had friends who lived close by, if he threw a football on the lawn to his friends in the neighborhood and if his friends he grew up with and wrote about lived in the houses we are driving by.

We look closely at the map and realize we are here. My dad parks the car and I run out to see the house. Before our eyes is a one-story house with flowers in the front. It is not modern and in an older neighborhood but somehow it looks like it twinkles with mischief! It really is so captivating. I notice my dad taking a long look at the house. He remarks that it reminds him of his house when he was growing up and he wondered if Jean Shepherd's family fought with the house furnace in the winter's freezing cold!

The outside of the house has an old fashioned feel to it. We find ourselves just standing there on the street and admiring it. I stare at the front door and cannot help but wonder if little boy Jean Shepherd stood on his toes to twist the door knob open. Did he run barefoot across the lawn in the summer? Did he ever have the taste of soap in his mouth? I turn around and catch one more glimpse of Jean Shepherd's boyhood house before I walk to the car. I grin. I cannot help but see a little boy sledding down hills in the winter. Wow! I can almost hear his happiness fill his pages!

Jean Shepherd is especially popular around Christmas. We watch the movie at our house over and over again because we love it so much! For me, I always tend to see myself in the movie because it is the way the movie is. You cannot help but see yourself in the movie and in his writings. I think that there are huge ties between Hammond, Indiana where he grew up and the movie. You feel as if you are part of his life when you see the outside of his house. I cannot explain it. I just feel like I knew the person that lived there as I stand here looking at his boyhood home. I knew the little boy. He was my friend. We celebrated Christmas together! Funny how movies can make you feel like that; books can make you feel like that, too. You read about someone and you feel as if you have just stepped into their story! I don't know what it is exactly but you feel as if you have just stepped into their life!

Thank you Jean Shepherd for making me so happy! I know there are millions of kids out there so filled with happiness by your work! Thank you for being a great writer and filling the world with your magnificent stories! But, most of all, thank you for feeding a little boy's creative mind! Yes! Your work tests one's feelings and instincts in the most enjoyable way! Jean Shepherd was many things. He was on radio, he was a humorist and of course an author. But after seeing the movie, A Christmas Story, I really cannot help but feel that Jean Shepherd was my friend. Wow! He really wrote with some great friendship skills! I think there is something else that is very interesting. Jean Shepherd wanted his readers to feel as if they were experiencing what his characters did in the book. And I want my reading friends to feel like they have joined me on my 200 national park tour and cool stuff along the way! I want everyone to feel like they are sitting in the backseat with me!

So, let's hop back in the car. Bring your ear-to-ear grins with you! Wave goodbye to Jean Shepherd's boyhood home! Looking at Jean Shepherd's boyhood home just makes you feel like Christmas no matter what month it is! Driving off to our next adventure, we are definitely a car full of smiles! Thanks for coming! See you tomorrow!

Your Friend Always,
Aida

Smiling makes friends~

Aida Frey

THOUGHTS ON FRIENDSHIP

Hey There!

I think this is a great time to talk a bit more about friendship! I think that the first thing a kid sees about another kid is their smile. So you if you want to meet another kid, you should have a nice smile. You should be friendly. I really do believe that smiling is the best way to start your day. It is a small thing to do really, but a smile has great effects! I want to tell you an interesting story.

On the second day of school, I was sitting at the lunch table alone because I didn't have any friends yet; I had just started high school. These two girls came and asked if they could sit down next to me at the table and I said ok. They kept showing a picture of someone back and forth and I caught a glimpse of the picture. It was Louis Tomlinson from my favorite group One Direction. Like the fourth time they showed it, I said "that is Louis Tomlinson from the group One Direction." And they said "yes"! They asked me if I liked One Direction and I said YES! After that, I was included in their conversation. We were laughing and talking. We all realized that we had something in common and we liked the same band. We kept talking about them and the rest is history and we became very good friends. One of the girls is at my bus stop. She lives so close to me I could walk to her house. So we have this in common. On the third day, we saw each other at the bus stop. Now, we take the bus together and sit next to one another all the time. I think having the same commonalties, liking the same things is a big part of friendship. But on the other hand, you don't have to have all of the same interests.

You just have to enjoy someone's company, enjoy their personality and be able to laugh with them! We met one another because of a band we both liked. So have self-confidence. Speak up! Don't just sit there! If you say something, you may just make a friend.

Wait! I just remembered a story about a different kind of friendship. It was at Assateague Island in Maryland. Actually Assateague Island is two parts. There is the Maryland part and the Virginia part. The Virginia part has the Chincoteague National Wildlife Refuge and the Maryland part contains the National Seashore and State Park. It is beautiful with beaches and there is even a lighthouse. Lighthouses are awesome!

Anyway, wild horses are well known here. I had an apple slice with peanut butter on it in my hand that my mom had made for me. Picture this! The slice of apple with peanut butter on it was in my hand but not for long! A wild horse came up out of nowhere, stuck his head through our open car window and snatched it out of my hand, right out of my hand! It was so cool. Like, how did it see me? Where did it come from? It was a beautiful sudden burst out of nowhere. I have never seen anything like it! It had been watching me. It must have sensed that I was a friend and it didn't have to be afraid. It was a very beautiful moment for me. I am glad peanut butter blows in the breeze!

I hope everybody had a great time today! I sure did!

Aida

THE MICHAEL JACKSON HOUSE

Gary, Indiana

Hey Everybody,

I remember how awesome it was to sit in front of Michael Jackson's boyhood house! Wow! Sitting in front of his house, I remember I felt like I knew the little boy inside the house eating his cereal, playing ball outside, joking around with his family. I felt so special just sitting there in the car. Wow! Seeing Michael Jackson's house when he was a kid. It was such a totally amazing feeling!

It was not very pretty from the outside. It was small and very lonely looking. But the little house was hardly a secret. And I remember that I so wanted to run up the walkway, turn its front door knob, open its door and hear its story. I so wanted to know about the little boy inside. I wanted to know who taught him how to tie his shoes and button his shirt.

My parents and I drove up to the Michael Jackson house in Gary, Indiana listening to Michael Jackson's hit, *I'll Be There*. We had driven the length of the block. The house was so still and quiet when we pulled up. It felt old, maybe older than it was. I don't know. But after a short while I remember saying to my parents that the house looked like it wanted to jump up and hug us. It was lonely, but it seemed somehow to have a joker-smile to it!

I got out of the car and then stood back and looked at it. You have to understand that to just look at the house and think that little boy Michael Jackson, well, that this was his house before the world knew him gave me butterflies. This little house had little boy Michael Jackson

47

all to itself but then like a bird, it released him to his window-tinted limousine and his stage performing star-studded life!

I remember signing the memorial wall outside of the house. I wrote "I love you Michael. You will always be the world's King of Pop!" Getting back in the car, we slowly drove away thinking about Michael's early days and his streak of extraordinary success. He had so much success in such a short life. The song *I Want You Back* plays. I looked back at the house and smiled. The house that I first thought was not very pretty when we drove up had done a costume change and reminded me of The King of Pop's doo-wop classic song *Little Bitty Pretty One*!

Aida

A CHRISTMAS STORY HOUSE

Cleveland, Ohio

Hey Everybody!

(Yawn) I must have totally slept through the rest of Indiana because we were in Cleveland a half mile from the Christmas Story House. When I awoke, I must admit that I have always been very comfortable falling asleep in the backseat of my parents' car. Cozily dozing off, I recall cuddling Tom (my stuffed fox) like he was a gift under the Christmas tree. I was so excited about seeing where they filmed this movie. It really started to feel like Christmas in the car!

I want to say that my dad has been a huge fan of A Christmas Story since it first was released. I personally think it is his favorite movie of all time. Of course, I am crazy about the movie too and so is my mom. We all love it! So, you can see what a thrill it is for us to actually go to the house where it was filmed!

After making a few more twists and turns, we found ourselves in a regular neighborhood of tree-lined streets. It was quiet. Looking back on that street, it could have been the background setting of a story. I looked at the street. My instinct told me that we were definitely here. I was getting so excited I could hardly sit still in the car.

I just remember how impatient I was waiting for my dad to park the car. The car bumped the curb and we parked. I was a nine-year-old kid opening the door and running up the steps of the Christmas Story House. I was a kid bumping against the cold with an ear-to-ear grin! I remember standing outside of the house and feeling like I was a kid in the movie. The house just made you feel that way.

The leg lamp was gleaming in the window just like in the movie. I was filled with butterflies! Waiting our turn to get into the house, I blew on my hands; it was so cold! My dad bought our tickets. The attendant ripped my ticket and gave me my stub. I stuffed it in my jacket pocket. The line began moving and I couldn't be more excited. The tour guide welcomed us. She ushered us in and I remember shouting out "Wow!"

You can't help but be struck by a smile when you walk into the Christmas Story House. There are many huge reasons why. First, as soon as you walk into the Christmas Story House it feels like the cameras are rolling. Really! It is like Lights! Camera! Action! You feel like you are actually part of the movie! It's really what makes up the experience. Every part of the story interacts with you in the house. You can feel every mood of the film. From the little porch outside to the steel mill in the back to the BB gun they used in the movie (I actually held the BB gun and it was awesome) to the soap, you are just fascinated by it all. Let me tell you about the highlight for me. The soap!

The Christmas Story House had a bar of soap displayed so you could actually experience this part of the movie. They even let you taste it! You might be thinking UGH! How could she! But, I wanted to really taste the truth of the movie! So, I closed my eyes tight, took a deep breath and licked the soap and do you know what happened? I got twinkling lips! Not from the soap, but from the experience! It was such a unique thing to do! I felt like Ralphie in the movie when he said the "fudge" word and his mom put soap in his mouth. Even though the soap didn't taste so good (why should it, its soap!), I felt so happy! I mean tasting the soap was a way for me to really feel like Ralphie and do something that he did in the movie! It was special! Yep! Even though the soap didn't taste good, licking it made me feel all happy and tingly inside.

I didn't want to leave the Christmas Story House. I wanted to stay! It was fun, fun and more fun. It was just so wonderful! It is like everything in the house just pops up like in the movie. It was so cool! And you are just a part of it all!

I remember I jumped into the backseat so excited and so very happy. I was so excited I couldn't sit still. Digging my hands into my jacket pockets, I pulled out my ticket stub from the Christmas Story House. Looking at it now, I still remember the steady stream of people entering the house. I remember the front porch, the steel mill in the back and how I licked soap! I will also always remember how a ticket so quickly torn in half gave me a wonderful red-carpet day and how the house made me feel like a star!

Hope everyone had fun! Hope you felt like you were in the movie!

Your Friend Always,
Aida

THE FLIGHT 93 MEMORIAL

Shanksville, Pennsylvania

Hey Everybody!

Flight 93 National Memorial is located in southwestern Pennsylvania and remains a very sad spot in my 200 National Park Tour. The memorial is within a 500-mile radius of two-thirds of the nation's population. I would like to take a moment of silence to pay tribute to those heroes on Flight 93 before I tell my story.

After the Christmas Story House, we were on I-76 driving through the backroads of Pennsylvania. Really, we were in the middle of nowhere and I remember wondering if this is how the pioneers felt. Of course we were driving through this wilderness unlike them. And I had my cellphone and I was taking pictures of the still life! Where were the tall buildings? Where were the supermarkets? Where were the fast-food drive lanes?

I really think America's creativity lies in those beautiful backroads. All you have to do is really just roll down the window and cup your ear and you will hear the outdoors in deep conversation! I do believe the trees chat amongst themselves! Real excitement was my companion as we drove deeper and deeper through those peaceful old back roads with the most amazing trees I'd ever seen! I closed my eyes as we glided alongside the smell of cedar. Opening my eyes, I remember being greeted by the most beautiful rolling hills you've ever seen. And I couldn't help but think I would love to get stuck to those hills because they were just so pretty! They looked like rolling bellies! After driving over the next series of rolling bellies, we entered The Flight 93 Memorial.

The Flight 93 Memorial is huge. There is so much land to the Memorial. I remember feeling so small in a place that was just so huge. I remember thinking that the land had to be big to pay a timeless tribute to the heroes who were on board that plane. I learned that day that there are villains in the world but there are heroes to fight them. That is what happened on Flight 93 and I think that that is what I felt the most while at The Flight 93 Memorial. You can feel that plane crashing down around you and your mind just starts thinking about the passengers. You start thinking about the heroes on that plane.

They made up the lines at the airport. Holding their carry-on suitcases, tagging their baggage, they became part of the airport culture, the faces of the terminal as they stood in line to board. The line probably moved slowly. Finally, their time came and they boarded as just everyday people, passengers on a plane to their destinations. Finding their seats, they placed their carry-on bags overhead. Probably everyone was happy that their flight wasn't cancelled. Leaving the gate, they taxied to the runway. Settling back in their seats, strapped in, they prepared for takeoff until these everyday passengers disappeared in the clouds.

I was sad at The Flight 93 National Memorial in Pennsylvania. The air was somber with a heavy feel of tears. I don't know, but I felt as if I wanted to grab a tissue from my pocket and wipe America's eyes. I sensed my dear friend, my country was crying.

I was only 6 months old on September 11, 2001 when four commercial airplanes were hijacked and used to strike targets on America's soil. Almost 3,000 people died. Flight 93 carrying forty passengers and an air crew were in the skies that day. If I was standing where I was standing at that time on September 11, 2001, the plane would have flown over my head. In tall panels of concrete, The Memorial lists the names of all the passengers, every one of them a hero. There were no survivors.

People who visit The Flight 93 Memorial can leave tributes in small niches in the Leave Your Message Wall. The following is the message we left:

The Frey Family, Chicago, Illinois: Flight 93 Never-to-be-Forgotten.

A sad day.

Your Friend Always,
Aida

Walking on the dam ... it was
as if the clouds were floating
around me~

Aida Frey

THE JOHNSTOWN FLOOD NATIONAL MEMORIAL

Pennsylvania

Hey Everybody!

Have you ever walked on a dam?

Can you imagine a wall of water reaching 70 feet high?

I will tell you all about it!

The Johnstown Flood Memorial was just under an hour from The Flight 93 Memorial. I remember the road sprawling beautifully before us. The weather was very nice as I settled into the backseat. The weather was pretty good. The weather was nothing like what happened to this town on their terrible day in history.

We had just had some great Frey travel food! Peanut butter and jelly sandwiches, celery stick munchies, fresh blueberries and apples with peanut butter. We love peanut butter! Also, the very best oatmeal and chocolate chip cookies come out of the Frey kitchen in Chicago! My mom passes me my juice box and my dad a can of pop as we travel deeper into the heart of Pennsylvania

Fortunate for me, my parents are great travelers. They don't get cranky or tired. We listen to music in the car and talk and laugh. It is awesome and our trip to The Johnstown Flood Memorial was no exception.

I think you have to get familiar with the countryside wherever you are. I think it is important to go beyond your city walls and get off of the couch, turn off your television, disconnect yourself from the Internet and really see America. It is important to experience things. There is a wider America out there that goes beyond going to your supermarkets and drive-thru restaurants. The natural beauty of America is like seeing one picture postcard after the next!

When I visit America's national parks, monuments and cool stops along the way, I feel like I am experiencing history. My parents and I enjoy touring the country by road and becoming acquainted with our past. We are touring America at our pace and it is awesome! When we are travelling like this, on the open road, I feel like I am on the road to the sun and the stars. I feel like we are just driving alongside a rainbow because everything is just so pretty. Driving past the trees, the greenery and the flowers, it feels as if the countryside is having a fashion show and I am looking at the latest fashions of nature which have been with us since the beginning of time! The flowers and trees all have their own star names.

Just when I wondered how it all could get any better, I saw a sign that said *Welcome to Ranger Country*! Oh Wow! If I could have done cartwheels across the backseat of our car I would have! I couldn't stop smiling! We stopped the car right then and there and took pictures. It was freezing outside. My teeth were chattering but I didn't care. My dad snaps a few more photos and I hop back into the warm car. Wow! The road we were on reminded me of a horseshoe. I couldn't wait to visit my new destination. We were at Johnstown Flood. What a great sign to welcome us! Too cool!

My dad parks and we step out of the car onto a soft grassy hill. Quiet and peaceful, scenic and surreal, it is wonderfully tranquil. We had no idea we were standing on a dam that had once vanished a city. It is here where I just want to stop a moment and talk about this. Can you imagine a city vanishing? Just completely swept away by water? It is hard to imagine. But this is what the Johnstown National Memorial is all about. It is about remembering the victims. This is all about a city that was just swept away by walls of water and few people believed it would happen even knowing it was built on a floodplain. But the dam did break. And like a tidal wave when the dam broke and the hills opened up, the water couldn't be stopped. Thousands perished and Johnstown was as if it never existed.

I think America changed on May 31, 1889 just the way it did on September 11, 2001 with Flight 93. Disasters make you think.

Whether they are on the ground or in the air, after days of relentless rain or after minutes in a calm sky, disasters create victims. After days of rain, the South Fork Dam collapsed and unleashed 20 million tons of water from its reservoir. A wall of water, reaching nearly 70 feet high, swept 14 miles down the Little Conemaugh River Valley carrying away steel mills, houses, livestock and people. At 4:07 p.m., the floodwaters rushed into the industrial city of Johnstown sweeping away houses and downtown businesses in a whirlpool that erased the town in ten minutes. On May 31, 1889, the town was gone.

I found a few things interesting. Both disasters happened in Pennsylvania. But in regard to Flight 93 as we understand it, in just over 30 minutes, they put together a plan and put it into action. The passengers stormed the cockpit and saved lives on the ground although they lost their own. The plane never crashed into The Pentagon. In the case of Johnstown Flood, they couldn't come up with a plan and so many lives were lost. The dam was not maintained properly. It rained nonstop for one week. The dam was already leaking. No one believed the dam would break. On May 31, 1889, after days and days of pouring torrential rain, The South Fork Dam broke and 20 million tons of water poured out from its reservoir and the trees began popping all over.

Both disasters happened in Pennsylvania. Both disasters have national memorials in Pennsylvania and both are in my book! I would like to mention just a few more things. Both disasters shared destruction of life. Johnstown was built on a floodplain. Johnstown flood took thousands of lives and Flight 93 saved thousands of lives. Flight 93 was taken by surprise and Johnstown Flood was warned over and over again of impending disaster and that the dam could break. Both disasters were man made. Johnstown Flood was not repaired and Flight 93 was an act of terrorism.

Goodbye Johnstown Memorial. I will never forget May 31, 1889.

Another sad time in history.

Your Friend Always,
Aida

CAMP WILDCAT CIVIL WAR BATTLEFIELD

Laurel County, Kentucky

Hey Everybody!

What could a kid possibly want after Hannibal Missouri? The Smokies! Yes! We are ready to take a jaunt to The Smokies! There is nothing like experiencing The Great Smoky Mountains National Park! It is so fascinating! It is so awesome! You can hike it on foot but you don't have to in order to enjoy it. Hiking is just one part of the wonderful things you can do when visiting The Smokies. There are so many short nature trails you can take and so much to see. Let me tell you about my Junior Ranger Story as we travelled to one of the most beautiful places on earth: The Smokies!

Bears were the word of the day in the Frey car as we headed to the Smokies. Yes! Bears, bears and more bears was the word! My dad learned two very important things on our road trip to the Smokies. Don't make promises and don't do night road trips anymore. You see, my dad wanted to save time and night drive to The Smokies and it was a great idea at the time when we were all comfortable and snug in our beds in Chicago. But once we hit the road, my mom was wide awake and she wasn't feeling too good. So after driving most of the night, Tom and me asleep in the backseat, mom wide awake in the front, dad turned the car off into a place to eat a very early morning breakfast. I remember him suggesting we make a visit to Camp Wildcat Civil War Battlefield as I was gulping my orange juice and he and my mom were drinking their coffee.

I could tell my mom still wasn't feeling like herself as she took a few bites of her toast and jam. However, her eyes did seem to light up at the Camp Wildcat suggestion. Leaving the early morning diner, we hopped back in the car. After a few twists and turns on the road, we found ourselves making an off-the-road stop! I think this is a great time here to tell you that my family and I make a lot of off-the-road stops! We see a sign along the road that seems like something that could be interesting and we will stop off and check it out! It is our roadside spontaneity that really is the secret formula for our road trips and, of course, our enthusiasm! We don't really stick to a schedule. I mean, if we see something that looks awesome, a sign that points to something intriguing, we are there! Do you know why? It is simple! We love cool stuff! So, we were on the way to Camp Wildcat on our way to The Smokies. My dad was promising bears again when we get to The Great Smokey Mountains National Park and my tummy was doing flip-flops I was so excited! I love wildlife so I was really feeling exceptionally awesome about the possibilities of seeing bears. But Camp Wildcat sounded pretty cool too and it was on the way and we are a family that doesn't want to let life pass us by for one second so Camp Wildcat it was! I knew we were on our way to something good!

We parked in what looked like a big parking lot. I remember literally flying out of the car on wings of excitement! My dad stopped to read some of the stuff on the information boards. He was looking at the hills and remarking about how quiet the trees were. He was admiring the wooded beauty of the surroundings. Everything was so green and serene. It was just tranquil and pretty and so very still.

The Battle of Camp Wildcat was the first Union victory of the Civil War and the first Union victory in Kentucky. It was really interesting to stand in the same space where the earliest major Civil War battle was fought. I felt like I was back in time, back in October 1861, when it was fought. And when you look out at the battlefield you cannot help but envision these trenches. By the way, a trench is a long narrow ditch and it is used as a shelter against enemy fire or an enemy attack. I don't know but for some reason I became lost in these trenches and the soldiers of the day digging into these trenches to save their lives. My eyes wandered across the battlefield, my mind visualizing these long narrow ditches dug by soldiers for protection. Somehow, I could almost see the dirt piled up in front of them in an earth shaped heap. Interesting, the trenches remain even though the battalions have long since been gone.

I had never been to a battlefield before. I want to tell you it made me feel so different. You start wondering what the weather was like, what those who fought were feeling and what they were thinking. Were they scared? How could you not be scared! Those boys fighting weren't that old. Maybe a little bit older than me?!

I don't know what it was but this battlefield just really got me thinking. I mean it was so quiet and it kind of welcomed my thoughts. In a sense it wanted me to think and feel all that happened here. And I did. It was almost as if it was inviting me in. The present serenity of the battlefield was so welcoming.

I could almost see both sides of soldiers trying to strengthen their positions, each side building trenches, digging in and fighting one another. The preservation of battlefields like this just really gets a kid thinking. You just wonder if you are standing in the middle of the fighting. You can't help but wonder what the thoughts were out here back then. This all happened so long ago and yet here I was standing in the same spot where a battle was fought and where heroes stood and died. I just don't know exactly what I was feeling. I'm wondering if what I was feeling then and now was freedom.

I remember looking over at my mom. Like me, this was the first battlefield she had ever seen too. I remember her pulling her sweater collar more tightly around her neck. I knew she was very moved by what she saw. Maybe she was hearing the final commands. Maybe she was seeing the final moments on this battlefield. Maybe she was seeing a lone figure saddled up in a wide brimmed hat, wearing a Civil War uniform rippling in the wind as the lone figure charged off to battle. Or, I wonder. Maybe, just maybe, she was just a mother feeling compassion, a sympathy of mind and imagining the fate of all of those sons on the battlefield and all the mothers who were left behind to smile at their sleep. My mom's eyes were shining. I think she was feeling better. Why wouldn't she feel better? She just saw history! Good-bye Laurel County Kentucky. Good-bye Camp Wildcat Civil War Battlefield. You make a kid and a mom proud. I hope everyone enjoyed Camp Wildcat!

Aida

I wonder if bears think we are crazy looking at them and snapping photos!

Aida Frey

BACK ON THE ROAD TO THE SMOKIES

Tennessee

Hey Everybody!

Hopping back in the car, we were once again on the road to the Smokies and my dad was bear-talking again. Of course I knew my dad's heart was set on showing my mom and me bears and I hoped we would get to see them. My dad would be so disappointed if we didn't see any. Keeping my fingers crossed, I hoped for the best!

From way back, when you are driving, you see The Smokies. They are soft mountains and they are absolutely beautiful. I am not kidding, they are so pretty! They've got this rounded look to them. They are not jagged peaks at all. They've got this rolling look to them and if you look at them long enough you think they are touching the sky. It is so cool. I wondered what it would be like to climb these big rolling kinds of mountains as they popped outside my car window. There were layers and layers of these rolling mountains and you just feel like you could jump from one to the other.

I remember my dad saying that The Smokies are super cool especially in the morning. You see, there is this fog that just reaches out to you. It is a thick fog and it just hangs over the mountains in the morning. The Smokies get their awesome name because of this fog that hovers over them that look just like smoke! Actually the name "Smoky" comes from this natural fog that seems to hang over the range like a constant mist. It is very interesting and from a distance, as you approach The Smokies, you see these amazing large smoke plumes. You have to see it to believe it.

I want to say something here. When I think of my visit to The Smokies, I believe it is this picture that sticks in my mind. But, more than anything, when I think of my trip to the Smokies I think it is the place where my dad learned not to do our road trips at night and not to make promises he may not be able to keep, no matter how hard he tries! I also remember The Smokies as the place where I got my National Park Passport Book! It is all coming back to me now.

You see, we had just checked into the motel which was two miles away from The Great Smoky Mountains National Park which hangs on the border of Tennessee and North Carolina. We were in such a hurry to get to the national park, we just dropped our suitcases on the beds in the motel room and then we were back in the car in no time flat. We just couldn't wait to see the Park and the bears! But the first stop was The Visitors' Center. Barely being able to see over the top of the counter of the center, I had asked the lady behind the counter for my own National Parks Passport Book. Standing on tip toes, I remember how I proudly reached for the book from the lady at the desk. Fingering its edges, I carefully put it in my knapsack for safe-keeping. Dated and stamped documenting my visit, it was six inches tall and four inches wide, slim and garbed in dark blue. I also got a National Park Passport Book for my trusted travel partner Tom!

The Great Smoky Mountains National Park is known to be bear country but it also is filled with log buildings which are really awesome to see and the most beautiful waterfalls in the world are there! You could just get lost staring at them. The amazing waterfalls appear along hiking paths that include the most gorgeous flowers that bloom all year along with magnificent streams and rivers. There are lush forests also. There is an observation tower that just tops Clingmans Dome which is the highest peak and offers the most picturesque views of The Smokies you could hope to see and what is even more, The Smokies are wrapped in a blanket of mist!

There are lots of trees next to the road in The Smokey Mountains National Park. It is so very green and clean and pretty. I wanted to get out of the car and just run around it was so awesome. How many times do you get to experience something like this? I rolled my window down. There was a wonderful smell of pine in the air! Just so fresh and beautiful! It was such a great day that I remember driving back to the motel with this gigantic smile on my face even though we didn't see any bears. I had a great time anyway.

I remember day two. We were driving looking for bears. We were searching mid-morning. My dad was feeling bad and going nuts because he had promised my mom and me bears and we hadn't even seen a bear-sighting of any kind. Hours and hours, back and forth, we went down roads where no one else was going. We were driving really slow, looking and looking. Black bears are the main attraction and we hadn't seen one. There were lots of hills and grassy areas but no bears. My dad was really feeling bad about it. We were all thinking that maybe the bears were eating a lot in October (which was when we were there) and they were getting ready for their hibernation. Really, I didn't know what to think.

I remember it was toward the end of the third day. My dad was going nuts on the bear thing. We were driving very slowly, listening and looking. I just felt that they had to show up. So I stuck my head out of the sunroof of the car with my camera ready. My parents were outside of the car. And then, out of nowhere, we saw one! We were just about to take a picture when a car came and scared the bear! The bear started running and we were off!

First my dad took off after the bear to try to snap a picture. Then I ran after my dad. I actually ran after my dad for two reasons. One was because I was worried about him in case the bear would turn and run after him! Secondly, I wanted to see the bear myself. So, once again here is the picture. My dad is running after the bear and I am running after my dad. The day was a cold one. I remember the cool air hitting my face as I was running after my dad who was not gaining on the bear at all.

My mom started yelling for me to come back. So I turned around and went back to her. Meanwhile my dad kept running after the bear and of course the bear ran faster than my dad. My mother was afraid of the mama bear. She was afraid that it would appear and get protective of her cub. After ten minutes, my dad came back without a picture. It was way too dark to snap one. There was no bear and there was no picture. My dad was very gloomy about this. His eyes were sad and sullen. Just as we were about to get back in the car, we turned back to look at the path where the bear and my dad were running. It was then that we caught a glimpse of the bear as it ran across the creek! Snap! My dad got his picture!

You know, after thinking about my time at The Smokies, I would have had a great time even if we hadn't seen any bears. There is just so much to see and so much to do! ! I have a plan the next time we go to The Smokies. I am going to visit the park just after sunrise and have my camera ready and just wait! Wildlife watching is amazing. Spotted owls, mountain lions, bears, deer, squirrels, falcons, birds are all part of the scenic ambiance. They have been around for centuries! You just have to be patient and experience. Go during the winter and you will spot them all a bit easier through the trees that have lost their leaves in one of the most beautiful parks that is on this earth!

I can't wait to see The Smokies again! Awesome!

Your Friend Always,
Aida

The greatest thing a kid can do
Is get lost in a double rainbow.

Aida Frey

NIAGARA FALLS & FRIENDSHIP

Hey Everybody,

My trip to Niagara Falls is a story of a beautiful adventure. It is filled with a double rainbow and a wonderful friend I made with a squirrel!

Niagara Falls is inspiring! It is world famous and sits on both sides of the border. I found it interesting that some falls are on the American side and some are on the Canadian side. Niagara Falls on the American side is a New York State Park and is a state park for New York but is not a national park. The first time we went to see Niagara Falls, it was raining cats and dogs and it was very foggy. The water that fell into the river was coming up with such steam you couldn't see more than fifty feet out. It was like a huge cloud of steam or fog. You really couldn't see anything. We climbed the stairs on the American side. Standing on top of the American Falls was very exciting for me. I was filled with oohs and wows because the falls were right underneath me! It is not often that you stand on top of Niagara Falls!

Let me tell you about my second trip to Niagara Falls. First of all, the weather was much better for us. We were welcomed by the most beautiful double rainbow you could ever imagine. It just filled my heart and mind with the most fascinating feeling and it reminded me that rainbows never end. Nothing beats a double rainbow. Nothing! It all started on The Maid of The Mist! I remember it well.

We boarded The Maid of the Mist, a Niagara Falls boat ride, and started off with the blue roof of the world over our heads. Maybe it was just being outside. Maybe it was being out of view of office buildings and concrete and the stuff that makes cities work. Everything that you are used to on a daily basis just vanishes as The Maid of the Mist takes you into the wild beauty of the mist. Hands over my face, I tried to protect my face from the powerful spray from the falls. It was the most beautiful mist-covered experience a kid could have! I loved every moment of it. I was filled with astonishment as The Maid of the Mist took us into the beauty of the Falls. Water was all around me. The crashing of the waves filled my ears. And then, the double rainbow! And I remember thinking that all this is nature's show and if I had to pick a winner, could the double rainbow outdo the crashing waves or the Falls themselves?! I don't think I have an answer to that! I remember thinking they all tied for first place because they all were so awesome! The natural world is amazing.

The Maid of the Mist has been running since 1846. It was so exciting from the river point of view. Nothing that I have ever done in my life even compares to it. If you want to go on the Canadian side, you follow the signs and you get up to the border and they check passports and and if everything checks out, you can go across and see the Canada falls. We went thru customs and crossed this huge big bridge and then we went into Quebec. We were able to go on the Canadian side. There was a casino over there and a big tower called The Skylon Tower. Really it is an observation tower and an historic landmark.

The Skylon Tower's outside elevator is huge. It is a glass elevator and it looks straight down into the Falls and the river. It is so amazing. What is really cool is as you are going up the tower you are able to see the Falls. There is a certain feeling that you are way above the earth when looking down at the Falls. Up and up and up you go to the 360 degree observation tower on the top. One or two floors down is a restaurant, right below the observation tower. We ate dinner there and as it was getting dark, we saw all the lights around the town and they have these huge colored spot lights that shine on to the Falls which was so cool and so very beautiful.

I had my ranger hat on while I was admiring the falls. Looking out at Queen Victoria Park, there were a lot of tourists. There was a squirrel and I started playing with it. The squirrel was following me all over. It was very nice! I walked out of the park and it followed me. I went back into the park and it followed me. One could say we were friends! Then a group of Japanese tourists began taking photos of me and the squirrel. I sat down and the little squirrel jumped on my knee and I fed it some nuts. The tourists thought that I was part of the rangers at the park! The tourists wanted to know if I took care of the squirrel at the park and I remember smiling and saying, "We are friends!" Niagara Falls is beautiful and is definitely a place of friendship! Just ask the squirrels!

Your Friend Always,
Aida

A great day is riding along
in the back seat
munching on an apple
& loving life.

Aida Frey

THE TUSKEGEE INSTITUTE NATIONAL HISTORIC SITE

Tuskegee Alabama

Hello Everyone!

It's a great day in Tuskegee!

The world turns to orange and brown when you visit The Tuskegee Institute National Historic Site in Tuskegee, Alabama. The campus is designated as a historical site which I found so awesome! It is a community of orange and brown. Everything looks like gardens and everything is so pretty. Maybe this is because Tuskegee Institute was really built brick by brick. The bricks and mortar were built from the land. Can you imagine they used the land to build the buildings? I just found this so interesting. I remember running all over the place to see everything. I didn't want to miss anything. I was staring at the displays, looking in microscopes and seeing how things were really done here. I was running far ahead of my parents. I just couldn't see things fast enough! Needless to say, I was having the time of my life!

It all started one day when my dad started talking about taking a Thanksgiving trip! Eyes open wide, a huge smile crossed my face! I remember him getting out this humongous national parks map. Spreading it across the floor of our family room, he started putting together this awesome Southern trip. I really do think that my dad could navigate the whole world with this huge map!

Sprawled out on the floor, I watched him put together our trip. It just totally blew my mind the way he could study this map and just like that, the most awesome vacation appeared! Concentrating, he diligently mapped out our trip into the wee hours of the morning.

One month later, we were heading south and leaving a freezing Chicago that was literally shivering in November chills. Now, one thing you have to know is that Illinois is a very long state to get through. From the top to the bottom of Illinois is about six hours. It felt like eternity and we were still in the great state of Illinois! Still, I was filled with excitement. No doubt the source of my excitement was seeing more national parks! I could hardly wait. I just could hardly wait! My dad was trying to keep it a secret, but as we were driving he let it slip out that we were headed to The Tuskegee Institute National Historic Site in Alabama and all I could say was "let the butterflies in my tummy begin!" And the butterflies came in full force as we arrived to a beautiful world etched in orange and brown.

Booker T. Washington was an amazing man. He guided African Americans with morale and skills. He raised their morale and let them know that they could succeed. His techniques were very powerful and filled with positive energy. He was definitely a pathbreaker. He was asked to join Tuskegee by Lewis Adams, a former slave and successful tradesman. Now it was Lewis Adams, along with another former slave George Campbell, who asked Booker T. Washington to come to Tuskegee and the rest is history.

Booker T. Washington came to Alabama in 1881 and began building The Tuskegee Institute. He recruited the greatest people he could to teach at Tuskegee and on his list of great people was George Washington Carver who, by the way, died at Tuskegee. I found it very interesting that under his tenure, Tuskegee became one of the leading educational institutions in the South. It provided a mix of teacher training, liberal arts and agricultural science as well as vocational education and training for elementary school teachers. It also attracted an international presence that was very much respected.

Tuskegee became a place of great wisdom for African Americans in the South in the 1800s. Looking like a little village, musicians, scientists, inventors and architects learned here. Tuskegee officially opened its door to former slaves in 1881 offering them a place to learn. Tuskegee remains a National Historic Site and remains a symbol of African American success and a constant reminder of Booker T. Washington's legacy in black education and culture.

Meanwhile, George Washington Carver was completing his master's degree in agricultural science at Iowa State when Booker T. Washington offered him the agricultural position in 1896. Booker T. Washington became its President. These were definitely two outstanding people at Tuskegee. No wonder why it became so great! Oh! There is one more very interesting thing I want to mention. George Washington Carver was called The Peanut Man because of his love for plants. He developed tons of uses for the peanut. The next time you eat sloppy joes with chili sauce or wash your hair with shampoo, remember George Washington Carver developed the use of the peanut in these products! How cool is that?!

I really learned a lot on my visit to Tuskegee. What really interested me the most was how the students made their own brick from the land around them and built buildings. But there is more. Students and faculty worked together to build their own buildings. I found this to be super amazing. I think Booker T. Washington's true greatness was he never entertained defeat. He pushed forward and I found my own attitude getting a push from him as well!

Booker T. Washington believed that teaching students how to be self-sufficient (to grow their own food, build their own buildings and make their own bricks) was practical and in this way, they would be qualified for practical jobs. He felt that everyone had to make a living and this was part of his program. I mean he had a business strategy and it was a very good one. His business philosophy had a very positive influence on black America. He was really a leader of black business development.

When you visit Tuskegee Institute you feel the pride and deep respect for higher education and for learning that is felt here. It is a place of adventures and achievements and goals and successes. It is a place of promises. More than anything is the winning attitude that I get when I think about my trip to Tuskegee Institute. A constellation of higher learning, Tuskegee brought the stars in the sky in reach to people who were taught to believe in themselves. Booker T. Washington and

George Washington Carver got students and faculty to work together, believe in one another and believe in themselves!

This beautiful and historical campus has created a sense of fireworks when it comes to learning. I felt a connection to history at the Tuskegee Institute. It made me feel curious about everything. It made me feel like I want to know about everything. I just wanted to stay there and research and learn. I guess I will have to wait awhile to do that. I'm not old enough quite yet! In closing, I do want to say that I am very curious about so much and am filled with a sense of learning. Not only has Tuskegee Institute had a global impact on the world, it has left quite an impact on this girl from Chicago!

Well everyone, I hope you had a great time! We are headed now to our next stop! See you soon!

Your Friend Always,
Aida

TUSKEGEE AIRMEN NATIONAL HISTORIC SITE
Tuskegee, Alabama

Hey Everybody!

Did you feel your ears pop?

We have just landed at the Tuskegee Airmen National Historic Site! This is a historic site that is really something so wonderful to see that you are going to think about it often. The museum is in the original airplane hangars of the training school. Not only do you learn a lot here, but it is so real you just feel like you are back in World War II with the Tuskegee Airmen!

The Tuskegee Airmen National Historic Site is just down the road from The Tuskegee Institute which you know now was a favorite stop for me. This historic site honors the contributions of African American airmen in World War II who fought the Germans in the air and fought prejudice back at home. The Tuskegee Airmen, known as the "Red Tails" because they wore these striped tails during their flight training, not only helped win the war but opened doors and opportunities to change life for African Americans.

It was a flying adventure for me the second I walked into The Tuskegee Airmen National Historic Site! It was so amazing! There was a little airfield and inside were all of these airplane displays. You could actually feel what it was like being in these planes when you hop inside of them! It was too cool! I felt as if I was inside a real World War II plane here.

The Tuskegee Airmen were some of the best pilots in the U.S. Army Air Corps. I felt so honored visiting The Tuskegee Airmen National Historic Site. It was a real high point in my life! What a great experience!

So, this is Junior Ranger Aida Frey flying the skies of World War II! I will be landing in Graceland soon! See you in my next adventure!

Your Friend Always,
Aida

Sometimes you have to
take a break in life
Put your feet up
Put your schedule aside
And just go with the wind.

Aida Frey

SHILOH NATIONAL MILITARY PARK

Shiloh, Tennessee

Hey Everybody!

So! We were on our way to Graceland when we put on the brakes! Yes! We put on the brakes! But, we do this. As you know, we don't stick to a strict schedule when we are on the road and there is something cool that just pops up and looks like it could be an awesome stop! I remember it as if it were yesterday when we were narrowing in on Graceland and my dad made an off-the-road decision and we detoured to The Shiloh National Military Park in Shiloh, Tennessee.

This battlefield is a very interesting one in southern Tennessee. It is a Civil War battlefield. It is where Union and Confederates are buried. Established in 1894, it famously preserves the scene of the Civil War. Shiloh is thought to be one of the best preserved battlefields in America and illustrates a war that lasted two days. Big and quiet, you just stand there and think about history and all that you are seeing. It is very moving. Today, this battlefield is a beautiful green place of monuments.

Now, something very cool happened to me at Shiloh. It was late afternoon and I was standing outside of The Visitors' Center when a lady ranger came up to me and my family. She wanted to know if I would like to help her take the American flag down and help her fold it properly. Oh wow! When I think back at this moment, it was such a cool thing for me to have the chance to do! I mean, how often would I ever get to do something like this?! It is about honoring the flag at the end of the duty day and I was so honored to be able to participate in doing something like this.

Eagerly, I watched the ranger and then helped. I learned it was a lot more to raising and lowering the flag. It was a huge honor! You see, it is about caring for the flag and signaling the end of the duty day. Flag duty is a real honor. I think when you are assigned to flag detail you are really filled with pride. I know that I was filled with this great feeling of pride as I carefully helped fold the flag of my country! What an honor! What a day at Shiloh!

Your Friend Always,
Aida

CHICKAMAUGA & CHATTANOOGA NATIONAL MILITARY PARK

Lookout Mountain
Georgia, Tennessee

Hey There!

Okay everyone, we are not going to Graceland just yet. But soon! I promise!

Today, I cup my ear to the stillness. It is all calm and quiet. But as I look out across this battlefield I am swept up in The Battle of Chickamauga which was in Georgia. The battle was fought on September 19th and 20th in 1863. I know it sounds crazy but I am lost in this battlefield. Why, I can almost hear the cannons being fired.

I remember it all seemed so real. Standing there, I felt as if I went back into the pages of time and that I was reliving history. I felt that I should be saluting my superiors and heading off toward the tents that had been set up for the soldiers. This battlefield somehow awakened me for I am among the many generations that follow it. There was this tower that I climbed up and looked out at the battlefield from the tower. I felt like I was in the clouds looking out at this battlefield. There were trees and grass and it was very peaceful. It was a beautiful scenic spot. And there is more! Come with me while I cup my ear to the stillness that surrounds me.

Chickamauga and Chattanooga are both civil war battlefields. Both Chickamauga and Chattanooga are National Military Parks, located in northern Georgia and eastern Tennessee. They both preserve the sites of two major battles of the American Civil War which were the Battle of Chickamauga and the Chattanooga Campaign. Now how did I get to these two places? Well, they are both managed by The National Park Service and were part of my 200 National Park Friendship Tour. Something I found very interesting is that Chattanooga and Chickamauga are both the biggest and oldest of America's Civil War Parks. Both commemorate the 1863 battles for Chattanooga that etched a huge turning point in The Civil War.

I loved every moment winding around Lookout Mountain. The higher you go, the more beautiful the scenery. Winding around the mountain, the two-lane road became even more winding. The scenery was even more and more beautiful with every turn. It was really so pretty. Old historical cannons, anchored onto the ground awaited us up at the top of the mountain. I wanted to cover my ears because it looked as if the cannons could go off at any second. The view was so beautiful from the top of Lookout Mountain. It was so cool to look out at the river. I felt like I could just settle into a lawn chair and look out at the world for a long time and listen to the world and its gurgling streams!

People live on this mountain. There were houses and I thought about what it would be like to leave Chicago and live in one of these houses. I found this to be so cool! I found something else that was absolutely amazing and that was way up at the mountain top was the battlefield. They had a civil war battle up there and it was called The Battle of The Clouds. Chattanooga is sometimes clouded in the mist and as I watched our car get swallowed up in the mist I felt like a little girl sitting in the clouds.

There are monuments and cannons at the edge of the mountain. Out of nowhere I decided to jump out onto a rock! (Hey! You are only a kid once!) I was wearing my ranger hat. People were picking flowers and they stopped when they saw me with my hat on! I guess I must have looked like some sort of authority! They looked at me like they respected me. It was a very good feeling!

Chattanooga and Chickamauga really are two battlefields that are combined as one national battlefield. They are only fifteen minutes away from one another by car. We decided to make the fifteen minute drive and go to Chickamauga Battlefield on the Georgia side. This was a very memorable place for me. It was there where I saw a picture of a girl who received some national park badges. She was being recognized for being a Junior Ranger. I don't know what came over me, but I wanted to have more badges than this girl! I really wanted to become active with The Junior Ranger Program!

It is here where I realized that I was a competitive person. I saw this girl's picture with the badges and it was a milestone moment for me in my life. It was a very big deal for me and that is all I can really say about it. Sometimes you just have to follow your heart! I wanted to have more badges than this girl. I wanted to be successful as a Junior Ranger. This is where my story really begins with The Junior Ranger Program. This is where I decided I wanted to visit the national parks and earn my badges by visiting America's national parks. I wanted to fill out my Junior Ranger booklet and earn my badges. This trip was so important for me. It was so monumental for me in my life. It was where I realized a little bit more who I am in life! And now here I am sharing my book about my 200 National Parks Friendship Tour with you! Life is great!

Your Friend Always,
Aida

I am with my inseparable friend, Tom at Little River Canyon National Preserve in Alabama.

I am with my good friend National Park Service Director Jonathan Jarvis in Washington D.C.

At beautiful Bryce Canyon National Park in Utah.

My Grandma and I, at Grand Canyon National Park getting our
Junior Ranger Badges (This was Grandma's first Jr. Ranger badge)

I was invited to Indiana Dunes National Lakeshore in Indiana as a special guest during their Jr. Ranger/Green Gary Days event.

I found this giant Smokey the Bear statue in International Falls, MN.

Fort McHenry National Monument and Shrine in Baltimore
is the birthplace of the Star Spangled Banner.

Castle Clinton National Monument in New
York City has a lot of history

I'm at Fire Island National Seashore with my Junior
Ranger vest and badges. They are so heavy!

Allegheny Portage Railroad National Historic Site is very
special to me because this was my 200th National Park

There is something magical
about Graceland.
It shows dreams can come true.

Aida Frey

GRACELAND

Memphis, Tennessee

Hey Everybody!

Yes! Finally! Graceland! See, I told you we would be getting here soon!

I really do believe that there is no place on this earth like Elvis Presley's Graceland. It is so amazing. The former home of the King of Rock and Roll, Mr. Elvis Presley is a gifted treasure not only for Elvis Presley but for Elvis admirers all over the world. Elvis was like no other person. He changed music and changed the world!

Elvis was an experience and Graceland was no exception. I remember seeing the big bus coming to take us up to the steps of Graceland. It was so exciting. The closer we got, the bigger Graceland got! I just kept imagining what it would be like to go to the market and come home to a place like Graceland! But it wasn't just me that was in awe of it all, my mom was just in awe of approaching Graceland as well.

My mom was born in El Salvador and she heard all about Elvis Presley there. My mom was very excited at seeing Graceland and visiting his birthplace in Tupelo which is coming soon. She was just as excited about The King of Rock and Roll as me! Somehow, you just don't think that you can like anything music-wise like your parents, but it just goes to show that Elvis touched my mother's heart and mine. If you are an Elvis fan you have to go to Graceland. It is a MUST! Graceland gives you a close-up view of the legend's life. It also gives you a close-up picture of his soul.

When you first walk into Graceland and you see it up close, you just can't help but shake your head. You see, Elvis was born into extreme poverty. Graceland is a place of magnificence. I walked into the various rooms and looked at the way it was decorated and all the things that were Elvis. Elvis really made it in the best of ways! Graceland is like something you've just never seen. Graceland preserves Elvis' grandeur. It tells the story of what he became.

I found it very interesting how protective the people who run Graceland are. They do not allow tourists to use flashes when you take a picture. Flashes over time damage the couch or chair fabrics, the costumes that you see that he wore as well as other things that made Elvis who and what he was. I really enjoyed seeing Elvis Presley's costumes. Elvis loved jets, cars and motorcycles! He was fun! He loved go-carts and dune buggies and pedal cars! I loved the Jungle Room. It was a favorite room for Elvis as well. It reminded him of his vacations in Hawaii! There are hundreds and hundreds of music icons, but Elvis is really an experience. I think Elvis has inspired so many music artists today. Elvis is historically significant and he had a huge love for America's national parks! Elvis Presley's life was a musical journey. Visiting Graceland makes you feel like you were part of his life! I liked walking where he walked and seeing the things he saw. And, of course, the greatest thing about Graceland was being with my family and my mom and me enjoying our love for Elvis together!

I think the very interesting thing about Graceland is that it still has its charm. Yes! After all these years, it has this pleasantness about it that just makes you feel good when you are there. People gravitate to it because they still love Elvis and always will. Elvis Presley was a success. He was born poor. Elvis Presley was self-made and changed the world!

I think Elvis also brought a beautiful spiritual beauty to the world. There is a special outpouring of prayer at Graceland. You can sense Elvis and his spiritual beauty when you walk through the rooms of this mansion. He attended church often as a boy and you can just feel his spiritual love at Graceland. Elvis Presley's spiritual beauty sets the tone for so much of his music. I think it is a very important part of what made him The King!

Elvis Presley, you remain an inspiration.

Your Friend Always,
Aida

My feet can talk!
And I wonder
Is it a magic pen or
Do I have magic feet?!

Aida Frey

LET'S TALK ABOUT SOLE WRITING
IF OUR TOES COULD TALK

Hello Everybody!

Hello is the most common greeting in the English language. I bet hell-o is heard every minute of the day! The word "hi" is a shortened version of hello. I say hello or hi to all of my friends at school, when I am on the phone, to my relatives and to my family. I am always greeting someone at America's national parks as well as the cool stops we make along the way with hi or hello.

I became curious about the word hello since I think that this word is a very big part of friendship. I mean it is the first thing that we say when we make a new friend. I have heard many things about the word hello. I would like to talk about an amazing story I learned about the word hello. I understand that the word hello dates back to around the time of the invention of the telephone in 1876. But, I also heard that the word hello was used in writing "Roughing It" by Mark Twain in 1872. What I found really awesome about this is that Samuel Clemens (Mark Twain) is such a favorite author of mine! And to think that Mark Twain may have used the word hello in his work before the invention of the telephone really made me smile. So, let's just casually say that the word hello came into existence in or around the mid 1800's. History is just so fascinating!

Mark Twain has had such a positive effect on me! I loved painting the fence when we went to Hannibal and somehow experience the pranks and good fun that Huck Finn and Becky Thatcher and Tom Sawyer all had together. So, I decided to be a little bit of a prankster myself in the backseat of my parent's car. It all began on our way to the Natchez Trace Parkway which was on our way to Tupelo, Mississippi, Elvis Presley's boyhood town.

Bored in the backseat on our trip to The Natchez Trace Parkway (which I will be telling you about shortly), we were on I-55 when I got this great idea! I remember it as if it were yesterday. I got this gleam in my eye and this smile spread across my face. My tummy was getting all hoppy inside! It was like this glow just seemed to engulf me and I remember joking to myself, let the fireworks begin! Grabbing my red felt pen from my knapsack, I tickled my feet with a bit of sole writing and wrote in big letters the word HI! Then I put my bare feet up to the window and people began pointing and laughing and smiling! Once again, my parents in the front seat were the last to know! It was like my vampire teeth experience all over again! Hey! You are only a kid once! Wonder what Tom Sawyer and Becky Thatcher and Huck Finn would have thought of this one! I bet author and humorist Mark Twain (Samuel Clemens) would have had a good laugh!

Your Friend Always,
Aida

I wonder if nature knows how beautiful it is!

Aida Frey

THE NATCHEZ TRACE PARKWAY

Alabama, Mississippi, Tennessee

Hey Everybody!

Do you love to see beautiful scenery? Are you ready to have a great time? What are you waiting for? Let's go to The Trace!

The Natchez Trace Parkway, also known as The Trace, is a National Parkway in the southeastern part of the United States. It is a very long roadway from Natchez, Mississippi all the way to Nashville. It is a 444-mile drive through what I call postcard territory! Everything looks like it should be on a postcard! It is all so picture perfect! If you love camping or biking or horseback riding, you can do all this as well. We drove and enjoyed every moment of it! I love history so I enjoyed seeing old parts of The Trace. There is much to see here. The Trace is made up of stories that span the centuries. There are structures that date all the way back to the 1780s along The Trace Parkway. And of course, we cannot forget about the old historical trappers and traders and boatmen and farmers and their battle through swamps and rivers, a terrain that proved to be obstacles for them and their travels.

The one thing that I would like to share with you is my story at The Trace. I still giggle about it. It all happened when I was walking around wearing my Junior Ranger hat. It feels like it was yesterday when I talk about it and it still brings a huge smile to my face. You see, it all started at The Visitors' Center. It was the first time that I put on my Junior Ranger hat.

My parents and I were walking along The Trace. We were walking along a path that people walked along centuries ago. I was feeling very important and happy and I was just filled with this wonderful sense of pride. The path was grassy and u-shaped. Walking along, we came across a Chickasaw Village. It was amazing. There were signs welcoming us to the heritage area. They celebrate their heritage with stories of their culture. Well, we were walking to the village when we came across a little kid running around and playing with a very big stick. He was banging the stick around on public property and creating a disturbance. Then he was hitting the trees with the stick.

I walked over in his direction. The little boy saw me with my Ranger hat on and he ran away. Well, let me tell you something - - - my hat was probably bigger than me! I suppose he thought that I probably was a Ranger and so he ran off. I remember standing there thinking that this was the first time that I looked like an authoritative figure. It was a very different feeling for me. Of course, I was very happy that the little boy stopped banging the trees with the stick. I didn't want him to hurt anything or do any damage to the beautiful surroundings of The Trace.

I never would have dreamed when I put my Ranger hat on that something like this would happen! Life is definitely an adventure! Speaking of adventures, guess where we are headed everyone! We are headed to Tupelo, Mississippi, the boyhood home of The King of Rock and Roll, Mr. Elvis Presley! But, before we visit Elvis Presley's boyhood town, I have a huge surprise! One of the Rangers from the Trace is coming up next in my pages! Wow!

See you!

Your Friend Always,
Aida

RANGER JANE FARMER

The Natchez Trace Parkway

Hello Aida!!

It is Jane Farmer from The Trace! It is so nice to be here in your pages!
 I have often thought if I visited national parks when I was a kid and Shenandoah National Park in Virginia comes to mind. I was eight years old when I visited it. I believe it was my first national park. I came from a very large family. We travelled a lot and we stopped in the national parks. We did drive a lot like your family does but I got car sick!
 Now that I think about it, I can honestly say that I was a dog and horse kid. But I also was an outside kid. And Aida, I don't think that I have grown up at all. I have four degrees in wildlife and fishery science but I am really still a kid and I will always be an outdoorsy person. Now what does that mean? It means as a kid I played outside as much as I could. I loved riding horses and still do! I loved riding horses though just like you like exploring caves. I really like volcanoes by the way. My dad was in the military and we lived in Hawaii. Hawaii is very pretty, beautiful scenery and trees and mountains and vast volcanic landscaping. I am a tree hugger and a nature lover also just like you! I am a fern feeler and just really enjoy nature. I find it hard to explain how beautiful nature really is. I just can't seem to find the words to talk about beautiful plants and explain the prettiness of it all! Getting people of all ages to connect with nature is really what it is all about.
 Aida, I think you are a delightful young lady. I love your interest in history and here at The Trace we have an awesome history. Enjoy the concept of America's National Parks! The national parks are for you and

everyone to visit and enjoy. There is a bonding element to the national parks. Bond with the plants, the history and the swamps and of course the wildlife! I didn't like history as a kid but as a ranger I embrace history and I embrace the land we live on.

Hugs to you for giving me the chance to step into your pages! I have had a great time! I will be looking forward to your next visit with us! Keep loving America's national parks, Aida! They are fantastic and naturally magical!

I LOVE TUPELO, MISSISSIPPI

Johnnie's Drive In

Hi Everybody!

Guess where I am right now? I am so excited, I can hardly eat! I am sitting at the Elvis table at Johnnie's Drive In! Yes! I am sitting in the same spot where Elvis Presley used to eat when he was a kid growing up in Tupelo, Mississippi and going to Johnnie's Drive In!

We had pulled into Tupelo, Mississippi and my dad drove us right to Johnnie's Drive In! He had this gleam in his eye. I could tell he was excited! Dad parked the car and we walked in and I could see, from the moment we walked through the door, why my dad was in such a rush to come here! The place was full of memories of The King of Rock and Roll! Everywhere you turned was history! There were stories and articles all over the restaurant about Elvis. The menu was on the wall along with more stories and articles of The King. You don't just read the stories and articles, you feel as if Elvis is there reading them with you over your shoulder.

It all started when we understood that there was an Elvis table, a table where Elvis used to sit with his friend when he was a kid. There were people sitting there eating already. So we looked around at Elvis' hang-out looking at all of the great stuff, my dad keeping his eye on the Elvis table! No doubt, the table became our destination event at this restaurant! And then the people got up and my dad made a mad dash to the table! Mom and I joined him in like no seconds flat!

The old fashioned touch of Johnnie's Drive In and sitting at the Elvis table made my imagination run wild! Why meddle with a design that has held up so well over the decades I hear my parents ask one another as we look around this diner-feeling restaurant. We sat at the table where Elvis used to sit. I remember feeling as if The King was actually sitting with us ordering his favorite cheeseburger and Dr. Pepper. Funny how the stage of a little table setting made me think of a ticking clock taking me back in time to when The King was a teen eating his cheeseburger with a good friend. It was an amazing feeling. No doubt, this table was a high spot event for us here at this restaurant of just a few tables where they don't take credit cards!

A guy came up to our table telling us how he used to sit here with Elvis and talk to him when they were growing up! Wow! I wanted to hear more about Elvis from his boyhood friend and I have a great surprise for you about this! Are you ready? I invited him into my pages and he said YES! This gentleman's name is Mr. Guy Harris and he grew up with Elvis Presley here in Tupelo. His mother and Elvis Presley's mother (Gladys) were very good friends! You will see Mr. Guy Harris in my pages very soon!

Munching my cheeseburger, my parents and I realize that this restaurant is very different. The menu is on the wall and the 1950's and 60's feel of this place is very impressive. You just feel that you stepped back in a very different era. I was just amazed to just sit here and know that Elvis was in this restaurant and maybe ordered what I ordered was so cool for me. I mean just being in this diner/restaurant with its memorabilia was thrilling! It was quite an interesting stop for this girl from Chicago. Why, I felt like I was dining with The King!

I remember when we were leaving, I told my parents' that I could almost hear Elvis Presley singing Jailhouse Rock. I wished I could have seen him perform and maybe he would have even asked me to join him on stage! Oh wow! Elvis was an important figure in America and all over the world. He brought many people so much happiness. And in Johnnie's Drive In you really feel so much of his life. I wonder what he talked about at this table. Did he come here after school with his friends? I wonder what his sense of mischief was and what were the things he did as a kid? Was he like Huck Finn and Tom Sawyer and Becky Thatcher with their sense of mischief? What were the things that Elvis the boy did as a kid? I wonder if he ever looked out the car window with vampire teeth in his mouth?!

Elvis Presley changed the world with his music. He was the new direction of his time. He had a musical chemistry with the world that still keeps the beat of today. I wish I could have met The King of Rock and Roll. I wish I could have seen him in concert. What a great day in Tupelo!

Get ready for my next surprise! You won't believe it! It's an interview with Mr. Guy Harris, Elvis Presley's boyhood friend and a true historian of Tupelo, Mississippi.

Your Friend Always,
Aida

MR. GUY HARRIS

Elvis Presley's Boyhood Friend

Hello Everybody!

We were everyday kids. We made our own toys. We made our own fun! We didn't have a routine and we didn't have a lot of money. So, we were up to being the wonders of a kid. You know, playing touch football on the lawn, that type of stuff. We came from a "yes ma'am, no ma'am" culture or suffer the consequences!
Mr. Guy Harris

"It wasn't about when I met Elvis Presley," said Mr. Guy Harris, Elvis Presley's boyhood friend. It was about when Elvis met me! Elvis met me in my mother's arms. I was just an infant. Gladys Presley, Elvis Presley's dear mother, and my mother were good friends. We went to church together. Elvis and I tossed a football and baseball to one another, read comic books, played stickball in the woods, swam in the creek and when we did have a little bit of money, we would go into Johnnie's Drive In Restaurant, eat a doughburger (a hamburger with lots of flour mixed into it). Sharing a table, we would talk about how pretty a girl was, talk about school and talk about how we were going to change the world!
Mr. Guy Harris (Mr. Guy) was friends with Elvis long before Elvis made a record. Mr. Guy Harris and Elvis were good boyhood friends who played at each other's house and enjoyed each other's mom's cooking! Mr. Guy pointed out that Elvis was born very poor. He lived the first twenty-one years of his life with nothing and the last

twenty-one years of his life with everything. Elvis, the King of Rock and Roll, died at forty-two years old. Gladys Presley, his mother, died at forty-four.

Mr. Guy was a friend and a fan of Elvis. He said that Elvis never stopped being his friend with all of his stardom and to this day, when he looks up into the hills, he can't help but see two boys roughhousing in the creek and dozing off on a mat of leaves.

We are headed right now to see where Elvis Presley was born and visit his boyhood home. You don't want to miss this!

Your Friend Always,
Aida

THE BIRTHPLACE

Hey Everybody!

The Birthplace is where it all began. Elvis Presley's dad built the house that is called The Birthplace. It is where The King of Rock and Roll was born.

When you go in the front door of The Birthplace, you will find upon entering, it is a square house. There is the front room and back room which is the kitchen and then a rear door. If you brought a shotgun to the door and shot it, the pellets would not have enough room to spread out before it would go out the back door. It is really just a very small house with two little rooms.

I remember we took pictures and when we left we walked up the hill and there was a museum, a beautiful statute of Elvis and a little chapel. My mom found the chapel very comforting and very peaceful. I found it to be very peaceful too. I want to say that The Birthplace and the chapel for me was an Elvis experience. The Birthplace is filled with Elvis the boy before he became a star and before he became a world icon.

Now, of course we saw other Elvis sites. We went to his grammar school. We went to the Tupelo Hardware Store where Elvis went with his mom in the hopes of getting a BB gun. His mom did not like this idea at all. As the story goes, the guy behind the counter tried to get Elvis interested in a small guitar, trying to convince him that it was much better than the BB gun. Of course this little kid's guitar ended up bringing out Elvis Presley's love for music, changing the world and the rest is history.

The Birthplace was very special for me. And I would like to take this opportunity to introduce to you a very special friend that I met along the way, Mr. Dick Guyton. There is no one who knows The Birthplace better than Mr. Guyton. He has given me a special smile. You see, I loved visiting The Birthplace so much that he accepted my invitation to step into my pages. You won't want to miss this next interview! Mr. Dick Guyton is fantastic!

Aida

MR. DICK GUYTON

The Birthplace

I am so excited. I am doing cartwheels in my pages! The Director of The Birthplace (the boyhood home of Elvis Presley) has accepted my invitation to be in my book. I am so happy! When my parents and I visited one of my most favorite cities ever, Tupelo Mississippi, we visited the Elvis Presley Birthplace and I was mesmerized as you know. I thought it was so amazing. The sanctuary was so wonderful. I couldn't take my eyes off of everything I was seeing. I just felt so wonderful being at the place that was Elvis Presley's boyhood home. I can't explain it. But, Mr. Dick Guyton gives his all every day to help make The Birthplace which is already such a special place, even more special if that is possible. Seriously, I am doing cartwheels! Let me tell you a little bit more about The Elvis Presley Birthplace and the man who runs it, my new friend, Mr. Dick Guyton. Before I go any further, I must thank Mr. Guyton for being in my book and for taking such wonderful care of an icon's boyhood home and for making me feel so at home at The Birthplace. It is a wonderful place to visit~

We still live in an Elvis culture and The Birthplace in Tupelo, Mississippi celebrates The King of Rock and Roll! There is no doubt that the memory of the little boy Elvis is kept alive by Director Dick Guyton's dedication to keep it simple and beautiful and peaceful and to keep it Elvis! The Birthplace is run by Director Dick Guyton who has managed Elvis Presley's boyhood home for thirteen years. Clearly, Dick Guyton loves his job and it is his love for his job that really keeps Elvis Presley's musical journey and memory alive and well. When we think of Elvis, we think of headlines and concerts and singing and dancing and guitars! But when you go to The Birthplace, you fall in love with the peace that Elvis has left behind and the sanctuary which seems to call his name to so many who seat themselves in the love that Elvis has brought and left to this world. Mr. Guyton says, "I meet people from all over the world." You never know who you will meet from one day to the next. Each day is different here at The Birthplace. There is a memory of the little boy Elvis here and his early life which contributed so much to his stardom. His early life and The Assembly of God Worship Service and how he worshipped as a little boy and the light of gospel were such a big part of Elvis and who he was. The church was a gathering place and a social place where everyone shared - - - dinner with one another on the grounds and a social gathering for country folk. Elvis, having so much talent, sang in the church choir. The church was a great influence for him and gospel was a big influence on his life. Having the church on the property shows his influence and gospel love.

It was very important for me to ask Director Dick Guyton what he was doing when he was nine years old. I started my National Park Friendship Tour when I was nine years old and so I wanted to know what he was doing when he was nine and he told me. Mr. Guyton was nine years old in 1948. His dad was struggling in a new business that he had opened. He spent a lot of time with his grandparents and loved it. They lived in the country and he loved being with them in the summer. He was there when they made fig preserves. Being around his grandparents, he grew to understand a lot and he laughed that he learned where milk came from. I think so many of us kids today don't even think about that stuff and we just take everything for granted. I found it very interesting that we both were doing something that we really loved when we were nine. It seems that we both were focusing on things that we really liked to do. I am doing something that my parents chose but worked out so wonderful for me. Mr. Guyton visited with his grandparents during the summer by the encouragement of his parents. I found that very interesting! Nine years old was a great age for me and a great age for Mr. Guyton!

I wanted to know more and more about Mr. Guyton. It was so interesting to learn that Mr. Guyton was not an Elvis fan until he started working at The Birthplace. Mr. Guyton had only been to the birthplace a few times until a friend of his called him and invited him to come to the birthplace and interview for the job as director. It was at this time that Mr. Guyton began to understand Elvis Presley's early life, his boyhood life. It was at this time he began to understand really what Elvis was all about. Working here, he sees Elvis fans come all the time and he sees what Elvis means to everyone who visits and he began to feel their passion, their zeal and their love for the man who changed and made music history. Gradually, he became a real Elvis fan. And Mr. Guyton is happy working at The Birthplace. He feels it is such a great place to be. He finds it amazing how one man, Elvis Presley, could tie everyone together - - - guys and girls, young and old, all people. Everyone recognizes Elvis in the same breath and Mr. Guyton realized this by working here. Clearly, Mr. Guyton is now an Elvis fan!

The Birthplace and Graceland enjoy a great relationship, each location being part of Elvis at different times of his life. The Birthplace preserves Elvis Presley's simplicity and Graceland preserves his grandeur. It is special people like Mr. Guyton who makes places like The Birthplace special and keeps places like The Birthplace special. Thank you Mr. Guyton for coming into my pages and telling me about Elvis and the birthplace and for telling me about you and your nine-year-old self! Oh! One more thing I would like to let Mr. Guyton know - - - my mom really enjoyed going into the sanctuary. She found it so very peaceful. She felt a warmth there and throughout The Birthplace. Yes! There is a peaceful feeling that welcomes you when you first step into the birthplace and it captures you just the way Elvis captured his audience. Elvis continues to teach us every day! Now, if I could only find a pair of blue suede shoes!

Thank you Director Guyton for this interview and for keeping Elvis' boyhood special!

Your Friend Always,
Aida

MAYOR SHELTON

I have an open door policy. If you are having a
problem with for let's say your plumbing and you can't
get it done, you come to see me
and we will get it done.

Mayor Jason Shelton

Hello Everybody!

May I present Mayor Jason Shelton~

Aida, thank you very much for asking me to be in your book. What
an accomplishment you have made at such a young age to visit 200 of
America's National Parks. That is a beautiful accomplishment! I have
heard wonderful things about you and I am so happy that you feel so
comfortable in Tupelo which is my kind of town! I know that you were
very eager to learn about me. So, let me do my best to tell you what I
was about when I was a kid and what I am about now. By the way, I am
looking forward to meeting you early next year!

Aida, one thing to know about me is I am not a "press 2" type of
a guy. It is also easier to bump into me on the streets of Tupelo than it
is to catch me on the phone! I understand that you like Elvis Presley.
Well, we have that in common, Aida. You see, Aida, I grew up as an
Elvis fan. Willie Nelson was the first concert performer I ever saw and
while growing up I always had an Elvis, Roy Orbison or Chuck Berry
record playing. My dad was an Elvis fan too! I must admit that I love
music but I cannot sing a lick and I cannot play the guitar and Aida, I
am not nearly as good looking as Elvis was!

I never dreamed of being a mayor when I was a kid Aida. I probably never ever thought about being a mayor! I was more interested in my bicycle and four-wheeler and fun things and making friends! I was just a typical kid into a bit of roughhousing, rolling around in the dirt and just being a boy. My life revolved around sports, pee wee football, baseball and just boyhood life. A lot of my boyhood life seemed to revolve around sports.

Today, as The Mayor of Tupelo, I am still filled with neighborhood pride and a huge connection to the city I grew up in. I grew up in East Tupelo and came to The Mayor's Office with down-to-earth and good old-fashioned Southern friendliness and charm. My dedication to being a friend to everyone in Tupelo is really what makes Tupelo work so well. I am dedicated to neighborhood friendliness and encourage everyone to take pride in their city. "I want the city I live in to be as great as the city I grew up in Aida! You know something about Tupelo? It is harder in Tupelo not to be involved than to be involved! It is just that kind of town!"

I really was very impressed with Mayor Shelton's open door policy. You can go to his office and talk to him. Mayor Shelton feels that most problems with citizens and the community can be resolved if the citizen can talk to the right person. And as for me, I must be the luckiest girl in the world! In the early party of 2016, I will get to meet with Mayor Shelton at his office, The Mayor's Office. Can you believe it? I can't wait! I will tell you all about it in my next book!

There is a natural friendliness that is part of this city. I really think that is what makes Tupelo, Tupelo! Thank you Mayor Shelton for stepping into my pages!

Your Friend Always,
Aida

P.S. You know, it was after visiting The Birthplace that I began to admire Tupelo. I liked Graceland. It was, to me, this huge mansion and it showed how you can succeed if you really put your mind to it. Graceland showed me that if you want to do something, you have to really try for it. Elvis Presley came from nothing and was a success.

Graceland shows what a success he was. But, The Birthplace really had an effect on me and I really like how Tupelo has taken such great care to preserve The Birthplace. I remember wanting to learn more about The Mayor of this great city and see, he is in my pages! You have to try in life. You have to always try!

I awoke one morning and my fear of caves was gone. It was replaced with a love for caves.
Now that's some kind of kid power!

Aida Frey

MAMMOTH CAVE NATIONAL PARK

Kentucky

Hey Everybody!

I am on the tip-toes of excitement! My smile is growing bigger and bigger as the line is moving to go into Mammoth Cave. My eyes grow wider as I step into the elevator with my parents as we slowly go down into the earth! I just have this feeling that this is going to be a super-eventful time. This is going to be good!

Down and down we go into the belly of the earth and I cannot help but wonder what would happen if a thunderstorm hit right about now and lit up the skies. Why we wouldn't even know unless the power went off and the elevator stopped. Really, I feel as if I am travelling through time as we are being lowered into the cave. I feel like I am going through old cities and past times. It's really so cool. And then out of nowhere, the elevator stops and the door opens and we are in the cave.

I take a deep breath. My nose is filled with the smell of earth. It's funny, but I feel extraordinary! I can't explain how I feel. The elevator makes me feel like I have taken a ride deep into the earth. I take a look at my dad. He looks like he is ready to get out of here. I don't think he is good with heights or being in a cave. I am fine with it all. I am an adventurist and it is all so cool. But I haven't always been this way. Back in my pages you will remember when I was in Hannibal, Missouri where the Tom Sawyer house was. I remember that it was very hot and humid the day we were in Hannibal. My parents and I drove to the Tom Sawyer cave and I remember my fear. I did not want to go in the cave. I was scared. I don't know exactly what my fear was. Maybe I was afraid of the dark. Maybe I was afraid of what a cave really is. Everyone knows caves are dark and filled with bugs (especially spiders). Maybe I was afraid of doing something so different. I mean it is not like you go into a cave all the time. I have definitely changed. But I think I have made myself change.

I don't ignore anything that is here to be seen. There is so much to be seen in a cave. Underground scenery is dynamic! Caving is amazing. Mammoth Cave is amazing. It is a cave that you can walk through and see different colors like brown and green and orange. It is so beautiful! It feels like you have left the earth when you are in a cave, but really you have just gone deeper into the earth. You get away from everything that you know. There are no supermarkets in caves, no skating rinks, no schools and yet there is a world of education. I will tell you something. Are you ready for a great secret about caves and a great secret about Mammoth Cave? Inside a cave, you can try to see how old the earth is! We always talk about how old we are, but we never think how old the earth is! The earth is so old we cannot fit enough candles on a birthday cake to celebrate! I think one day we should light millions of candles all over the country and then let the wind blow them out to celebrate the earth's birthday!

It is interesting to learn that the earth shifts and during one of the earth's big shifts, the land started to be seen above the water. Sandstone was added to the land masses and Mammoth Cave was born! Mammoth Cave came from rock transformations that happened a long time ago. So, when my parents and I were standing in Mammoth Cave and looking at the different types of rocks and ducking our heads from the low ceiling, we saw these transformations.

Mammoth Cave is a teacher. Yes! That's right! It is like a teacher and a school in itself. It teaches us about our culture and when there may have been interaction in this cave. I find this so fascinating because it is prehistoric and by now everyone knows how much I love history! But, really, even if you are not a history lover, you will find it fascinating. Now there is not a lot of light in caves. In Mammoth Cave, you don't need a lantern because it is lit enough to walk through because of the rock ceiling. Caves are so interesting!

I must tell you that Mammoth Cave is the largest cave in the world. So please don't think that you can see the whole cave in like one day. It doesn't work that way. You can't rush seeing a cave, especially Mammoth Cave! The place is full of secrets! There are secret passageways all over the place and some say there are even ghosts! Now one more thing to always keep in mind if you are going to be a caver and that is to take a sweater with you. Caves are usually cold. Remember, caves are under the earth and they do not get any sunlight. So bundle up!

Your Friend Always,
Aida

I will never forget winding our
way up to Lookout Mountain!
I remember feeling like I was
climbing a ladder above
the clouds!

Aida Frey

RUBY FALLS

Chattanooga, TN

Hi Everybody!

Have you ever seen a waterfall over 1,120 feet below the surface? Well, you are going to tour the falls, Ruby Falls, with me right now! Come on! Let's go and while we are at it, let's take a trip above the clouds!

I will never forget winding our way up to Lookout Mountain! I remember feeling like I was climbing a ladder above the clouds! Wow! What a feeling! What an experience! Ruby Falls is a cave on Lookout Mountain and is one of the top ten most incredible cave waterfalls on this planet! It is America's biggest underground waterfall by the way. It has a waterfall inside and I was just blown away when I saw it. Ruby Falls is 1,120 feet below the surface of Lookout Mountain in Chattanooga, Tennessee and filled with the most beautiful rock formations and gardens. The underground waterfall is always fifty nine-degrees inside so it is definitely sweater weather! Walking along through the most beautiful nature you've ever seen, you can look all the way down into Chattanooga. It is so beautiful! By the way, if you are wondering how Ruby Falls got its name, a gentleman by the name of Leo Lambert and a team of excavators found the falls and named them after his wife, Ruby!

Another interesting thing to tell you guys is that Babe Ruth visited Ruby Falls. As a matter of fact, Babe Ruth and Lou Gehrig, the two famous Yankees were doing this tour around The United States to promote baseball. There was a woman who pitched on some team in

Chattanooga and the promoters thought it would be cool if she pitched to Babe Ruth or Lou Gehrig. She pitched to Babe Ruth and she struck him out! Can you imagine that?! Well, one thing that I really found amazing was that I was at the same place as Lou Gehrig and Babe Ruth. I was right where they were and I remember it just made me feel awesome!

Now, Ruby Falls is on Lookout Mountain and it is way up there! So, my parents and I decided to do the INCLINE and see this spectacular view! So, we got tickets. This track is like a roller coaster and it goes straight down the mountain. I am telling you the truth! It was so awesome. The rail cars are almost straight down. And the seats are curved like so when you walk along the train they curve. So, the way you get in the seats are curved. It is so different. Now, it is not like you are falling out of the seats. They are straight when you get in them. Now, the one thing that I wondered was how am I going to get in these seats without falling down? My dad was kind of freaking out about it because he is not so crazy about heights! He looked at the seats and he had this look in his eyes like are you kidding me!!!

So we boarded and it felt like the biggest roller coaster ever! You can't help but look down. It was so amazing! Our car goes down and pulls another car that is going up. It uses a pulley system. The pulley system is using the car at the bottom to pull them up. The power is coming from the car going down the mountain. It is amazing. I wasn't scared at all. It is a bit crazy and I loved every single minute of it! It is like they created railroad tracks on the side of the mountain! How amazing is that! It goes very slow and it just feels like you are going straight down the mountain. You are looking down and down and down. The view was so awesome and was filled with lots and lots of trees!

There is so much to Lookout Mountain and Ruby Falls. There are homes all over Lookout Mountain. I would love to live up there! You can see these houses when you leave Ruby Falls and it is kind of what stays in your mind since it is the last picture that you see. I do want to say one more thing that I really enjoyed seeing was the top of Lookout Mountain and the Napoleon cannons that are up there. That really gives you such an amazing historical feel. You see, Chattanooga and Lookout Mountain played big roles in The Civil War. The Battle of Lookout

Mountain was also known as the Battle above the Clouds and I can relate to why they call it that. The whole time I was seeing Ruby Falls and just experiencing everything, I felt like I was a girl in the clouds! What an experience! What a great trip! I hope you had fun! I sure did!

Your Friend Always,
Aida

I WANT TO MAKE LIFE BETTER
FOR ALL ANIMALS.

I WANT TO BE PART OF THIS
CHANGE.

Aida Frey

ROCKY MOUNTAIN NATIONAL PARK

Colorado

Hey Everybody!

The Rocky Mountain National Park's 415 square miles encompass and protect the most beautiful mountain environments you've ever seen. I want to talk about this national park and an animal wildlife story. There is a lot of family fun in this national park and that was really good for us because our trip to this national park had us driving through it in a very tightly packed car!

I remember my grandmother and my Uncle Todd coming with us on our trip to The Rocky Mountain National Park. Cresting over 12,000 feet and overlooking the alpine and subalpine worlds, you feel like you could roller skate across the sky! We were driving along, overlooking the wildflowers and hiking trails and looking forward to seeing the starry nights when it turned dark when out of nowhere something so fantastically unbelievable happened. I mean, I really think that it just happens once in a lifetime, twice at the most! We saw these huge big elks outside of the car. They were so close to the car that if you rolled down your window you could reach your hand out to pet them. It was absolutely amazing! So, first we saw an elk on the left side of the car and then we saw an elk on the right side of the car. Now mind you, they were just a few feet away from the car.

Okay. So they began to look like they were going to fight. You know, they fight for dominance. Well, here we all are. My mom and my dad, my Uncle Todd, my grandmother and me! We are all in the car and in the middle of these warring elks! Oh my goodness! We just didn't know what to do! Now, I have a whole lot of love for viewing wildlife! I love wildlife watching but I am not sure my grandmother and my Uncle Todd felt the same way! I was very concerned what would happen if they started fighting with all of us stuffed in our car in the middle of their brawl!

Now, I know that elk can be seen all over the park at any time but a popular time to see them is during mating season. If you want to find elk, they tend to be where the forest and meadow meet. Elk spend a majority of their time around the tree-line during the summer, moving to lower elevations in the fall, winter and spring. The elks' favorite times to eat is at dawn and dusk. So, I began to think about what my dad had mentioned that it was a dominance thing. But, I also know that you have to know a bit about wildlife watching. If you are going to go wildlife watching, you need to always watch from a distance and a safe distance. You have to use binoculars or a telephoto lens to get close-up views. Following larger animals to get a photograph or a better look can make them nervous and stress them out to such a point that it could threaten their health. If animals notice you or the people that you are with are nervous, you are too close. Move away quietly. Well, this all sounded great, but when you are sandwiched between two warring elks, it is better to just let the warring elks call the situation because it wasn't like we could just drive away quietly enough. We were right in the middle of these two warring buddies!

So, it was very interesting to see wildlife and what comes natural. Both elks stared at each other for quite a bit longer and no one in the car was saying a word. I am still not sure to this day if we were all fascinated or if we were too worried to speak! The elk on the right which was the bigger elk of the two started to move off. And then the smaller elk just went hiding behind the tree. And then that just seemed enough for the bigger elk that his stare made the smaller elk hide behind the tree and so then the bigger elk just cleared out. I think all of us in the car breathed this big sigh of relief at the same time probably along with the smaller elk behind the tree who stayed there just a little bit longer to make sure that the coast was clear and then he moved off too. I'm sure that my parents' Impala breathed a sigh of relief too as my dad stepped on the gas and we slowly drove away!

So, The Rocky Mountain National Park is way up in the mountains. Driving away from our elks, we drove on to the narrow roads and wound above the mountains. Higher and higher we all went and then we saw them! Oh wow! We started seeing the monster 14,000 foot mountains! Oh wow! The mountains just stood out with their majestic grandeur! As we rounded the corners with their tricky turns, we began to see the snow at the top and I knew we were on the road to something really cool here! Up and up and up the five of us went in the car. Once again we all stopped talking when we saw the beauty of these mountains. It was so impressive. It really was America at its finest! America just looked so awesome. What a beautiful day with nature and with wildlife!

Your Friend Always,
Aida

Animals and Nature Have
Their Own Language
They Understand One Another
It Is People They Wonder About~

Aida Frey

YELLOWSTONE NATIONAL PARK

Wyoming, Montana, Idaho

Hey Everybody!

Yellowstone National Park is like a mega-star of natural beauty. It takes center stage when it comes to nature. Yellowstone's wilderness is atop a volcanic hotspot which spreads out mostly in Wyoming but into parts of Idaho and Montana as well. It is the home of the geyser Old Faithful as well as many more geysers that are preserved here. It is also the home to so much wildlife it is amazing! Yellowstone is loaded with canyons, forests, hot springs and rivers. And Yellowstone National Park is a big part of my awesome 200 National Park Friendship Tour!

We spent four days at Yellowstone National Park. I remember every minute of it and it was great! We saw Old Faithful, the most famous geyser in the whole world! I remember watching it and seeing how after a few minutes it blows and how excited I got when I saw it! I remember it was so cool! Let me tell you a little bit more about Old Faithful!

The day we went to see Old Faithful there were benches out for everyone. We found out about this so we got there early so we could get a good seat. The closer it got to the time for Old Faithful to blow its stack, the more jam packed the area became. Of course, it was jam packed and the excitement just began to mount every second. I could hardly wait to see it all. I was filled with so much anticipation I couldn't sit still. Let me tell you something, things really livened up when Old Faithful was about to blow its top!

I remember it was very sunny and beautiful outside. Everyone was glued to Old Faithful. But, Yellowstone's Old Faithful seemed to be aware of its popularity. It started out very slowly. You started seeing the steam come out of the hole on its top and everyone was just oohing as they were watching. And then the steam out of its top started to increase and get bigger and bigger. Then, you start seeing more steam coming out from the geyser! Wow! Then it goes to 5 feet tall and then 10 feet tall and then it really comes out like there is no tomorrow and people are just filled with amazement including me!

You know Yellowstone's Old Faithful has a story all of its own. People come from all over the world to see Old Faithful blow its top! It's great! But everyone who comes to see Old Faithful is not just its audience. Oh no! The audience for Old Faithful becomes part of its story. For decades and decades people have come to see Old Faithful. One wonders if all of the attention is what keeps Old Faithful blowing its top! I think Old Faithful feels loved! I know that as we left Yellowstone, I felt like I wanted to run up to Old Faithful and give it a hug! Yellowstone is a different kind of park. You see so many different things at Yellowstone. You see wildlife and mountains and valleys and lakes and rivers and meadows and lots and lots of forest land. There are a lot of geysers and hot springs and waterfalls. I love waterfalls almost as much as I love caves! Yes! Waterfalls are awesome but my favorites were the grizzly bears and black bears! Wow!

We were driving across Yellowstone and there was in a row little mounds of dirt and it was kind of hilly. There were lots of cars. They were stopping for traffic and I remember we were wondering what the hold up was and everyone got out of their cars. I remember out of nowhere two black bears ran across the road. The ranger didn't want anyone getting out. No one should get near the bears because the bears might attack them. My mom and dad and I saw the bears and we walked near the road where everyone was. And I am wondering where the rest of their family was. It seemed like the bears knew where they were going and all the people looking at them were stumped but I think that the two bears had it in mind just what they were doing. We also saw a pack of wolves and this was interesting because wolves are not easy to see in Yellowstone. On our last day at Yellowstone, we were driving south through the park when we saw them! We saw a pack of wolves. Oh wow!

We were heading to Grand Teton National Park. So, we were driving along and thinking we have a long way to go. We were not expecting to see anything and then wow! We saw a bunch of cars and only my mom got out of the car and she walked up to a lady to try to find out what everyone was looking at. And she was told there was an elk out there on the road. I remember the bushes were very thick. We were all looking and watching. I am not kidding about this. It could only have been a few seconds later my mom was screaming and running back to the car. There was an elk in my mom's face! It was a close encounter of the elk kind! My mom put her face right next to the bush and trying to look through the bush she looked eye-to-eye with an elk! This gigantic elk was five inches away from her face with its big rack of antlers! Wow! She was so freaked out. The elk was looking at my mom and my mom was looking at the elk. My mom was not expecting it to be there and she ran back to the car as fast as she could! I had never seen her run so fast! Of course after my dad and I knew that she was ok, we all started laughing about her close encounter with the elk kind! After a bit, my mom started thinking about it all and how funny she must have looked running back to us and how funny she must have looked to the elk peering into that bush which was his turf!

We saw a lot of buffalo in different parts of Yellowstone. When you are there and you see these things, you just want to park the car and jump out! My dad, of course, was always trying to take pictures of me with the buffalos or with any wildlife. The buffalo got really close though. We didn't get out of the car but I really wanted to do that! My grandmother and my mom emphatically voted me out on that one! The buffalo looked really cool.

So we were driving in the woods and we saw one big buffalo! Oh wow! We were driving next to this huge buffalo. It was right next to my back car window and it was so close to the car that if I had my window down, I could have touched it! Oh wow! I could have touched it! My grandmother and my mom were both scared of it but I wasn't at all. We took a lot of pictures from the car. We also saw wolves and there were wolves in the clearing also. We saw people with lots of cameras and they were taking pictures of the pack of wolves. We got our binoculars and we saw the wolves running. I like wolves. I love dogs and dogs are close to wolves and I just like them. I like their energy and I like the way they are. I like the way they look. I couldn't take my eyes off of them!

Driving once again, my dad and mom and grandmother are staring off out of the car windows into the woods. I am gawking out of my backseat car window, eyes glued to the woods before us. We had heard when we were taking pictures of the wolves that there was a moose spotted in this area of wooded country. So we were off to see the moose. There were tons of trees but I saw it. I saw these antlers and they were moving and I spotted the moose. After thinking about it for a few minutes, I wasn't sure if it was an elk or moose but I know one thing I loved it no matter what it was. It is really something to see wildlife! There is nothing like looking at wildlife especially when it is so that you can reach out and touch it! It is such a difference to see wildlife and nature and get away from the concrete jungle and shopping malls that we see all of the time. Nature and wild life are amazing!

There is no doubt in Yellowstone that you see a lot of cool stuff. There are places where you can see old grove forests and there are places where you can see five or six or seven feet tall forest trees and these are newer trees. These trees came up from the fires in 1988 so I want to share the fires of 1988. They had a horrendously bad fire season in Yellowstone. Awful. There was a huge fire because there was so much debris after years and years of dead trees and limbs falling. All this debris just sits there, old and rotted. It is highly flammable. And millions and millions of acres of dead stuff and live trees that had never been touched by a fire were burned when the huge fires started in Yellowstone in 1988. They could not control these fires. The fires burned up all the garbage of the forests and after the fire was out very shortly there were acorns and seeds from trees that had never burst open because they were there on top of all of this debris. Once everything was burned and all of these seedlings went down into the ground naturally, brand new trees and bushes came to life. They also breathed life, air and the trees and the garbage debris on the bottom of the floor started a new generation of trees and bushes and flowers. And in this case the fires were a natural way of restarting growth in a natural forest like this. It was really interesting all that nature is made of. Wow! Nature is so smart!

One more thing I want to talk about. In the badlands, there are the prairie dogs and in my mind I think these are dogs. I saw the prairie dogs and they look so different from dogs! They look like a beaver or a gopher or ground hogs. This was my first time seeing prairie dogs and so my mom was really astounded by this and I remember joking about taking a ground-hog home with us! It was a great day. Oh my goodness! They were really cute!

Your Friend Always,
Aida

P.S. There was a part of the woods that had something like a little farm and we got out of the car and I went out on this path looking for them. I stood very still so that prairie dog would come up to me. They are so cute and I didn't want them to run away. White prairie dogs are very rare by the way and I sure kept my eyes peeled for those guys. So I kept walking along the path when my mom and I saw the regular brown one. My mother was crazy about this and so we were giggling when we got back in the car how much is that prairie dog in the window!! Arf! Arf! It was a cool day at Yellowstone and it was a cool day with my family!

I SEE A MOOSE
AND I WANT TO TAKE A
PICTURE
I WONDER IF THE MOOSE
SEES ME
AND WANTS TO TAKE MY
PICTURE!

Aida Frey

GRAND TETON NATIONAL PARK

Wyoming

Hey Everybody!

I have another wildlife story to tell you!

We were heading south through Yellowstone. Now, Grand Teton National Park is in the northwest part of Wyoming and is linked to Yellowstone National Park by the John D. Rockefeller, Jr. Memorial Parkway. It is so beautiful. You can explore all types of trails and see wildlife. I remember feeling so adventurous because there is so much to explore and see and experience. So, let me tell you what happened.

We were driving along when we came to this huge field area with a creek running through it. It was enormous. We noticed that there were about fifteen cars pulled over. We stopped and then we moved forward and pulled over too. My mom and dad got out of the car to see what was going on. I got out too. People were out of their cars talking amongst one another. We kept hearing people saying that there were wolves feeding on a buffalo. Well, we got out our binoculars to try to take photos and see what was happening. It was exciting to everyone because it is an extra thrill for people driving through the park to see any type of wildlife picture. For me, I always want to see wildlife, especially bears, wolves and, of course, a moose or two would be awesome! I remember it was like a football field away when we saw three grey wolves. There was a dead buffalo in the creek and the wolves were feeding on the buffalo.

We were very lucky on this trip because we saw two bears and three wolves while at Yellowstone! It was so incredible! But I am not nearly done! There is so much more to this adventure! Listen to this! Continuing south, we drove along into the John D. Rockefeller Jr. Memorial Parkway. Now, this is a scenic road that connects Grand Teton National Park and Yellowstone National Park in Wyoming. It is federally owned and managed by the National Park Service. The Grand Teton National Park is a very big mountain range. It has the most beautiful rocky peaks you've ever seen. It protects all of the lakes, rivers and parks. There are a lot of visitor centers and we met five lady rangers who were very nice to us while we were there. The rangers were very happy to see us and they gave us an interesting lesson on the world that surrounds us!

The first interesting lesson that the rangers gave us was about the aspen tree. I would like to tell you all about it. Okay! Here goes! Back in the pioneer days, if the pioneers could find an aspen tree and the sun was out and it was very hot, they would rub their fingers on the tree and they used it as natural sun block! Wow! Natural sun block comes out from the aspen tree! I found this so interesting. You see there is a story behind so much we see in nature. The beautiful trees in the forest or that we see from the roads when we drive all have a story! In the case of the aspen tree, the pioneers were protected from the hot harsh sun from the natural ingredients in the aspen tree! And you see, we go to the store to buy our suntan lotion!

We began driving through Grand Teton after we left the rangers and we noticed a bunch of cars stopped. There was like this long road that looked like a driveway or a path. We were wondering why so many people were just stopped and then we saw it! You won't believe it! We saw this huge Bullwinkle moose! It was not far from us at all. So we parked the car like everyone else and we got out of the car and began snapping photos. It was very slow moving. It had these humongous antlers! Everyone wanted to be careful not to startle it. We wanted to keep it calm. It looked at us as if it was wondering what all the fuss was about! It was a great day for me at Grand Teton!

Your Friend Always,
Aida

HOT SPRINGS NATIONAL PARK

Hot Springs, AR

I am enchanted! I am just fascinated!

People come from all over the world to taste and feel the hot springs! The water is so popular! People from all over the world come to this health resort to soothe themselves in thermal spa waters and relax. Can you believe a city built up around hot springs? Nicknamed The American Spa, Hot Springs National Park is a popular place that surrounds the north end of the city of Hot Springs, Arkansas! And, what is even more, I drank the water!!

Tucked away in Arkansas is the most amazing national park! Hot Springs National Park is just surrounded by history. Its special spas and mineral water make it a precious place to visit. It makes no secret about its water wealth! From the second you walk into The Hot Springs National Park you know it is so unique. It is definitely a place for health, enjoyment and insight! I have never seen anything like this before. I couldn't believe what this place was all about. There were beautiful old and new buildings and lots of different colored flowers. This is a place that is known for its springs and its outstanding water. The water is so unbelievable you don't even feel it going down your throat. It kind of just melts in your mouth. The water is not only very pure, and really good, but it is free! Yes! The water is free!

It is interesting that travelling to spa towns or resorts is not a modern thing. Oh no! It goes way back in history when people have been in search of cures for the fountain of youth or elixirs that make them strong. Spas have been around since the dawn of history. Yes! It seems like there have been strong beliefs in the curing and healing effects of something as simple as water since the beginning of time. There was a time in history when the natural springs were thought to be blessed by the gods and these sacred spas were for those of royalty. The therapeutic use of water has existed from ancient times up to the present day.

There was a little fountain outside from where we were standing when we were there. We saw a family put like fifty bottles of the water in their car! We asked where they were from and they said from very far away. They were telling us that they made the trip to Hot Springs National Park every few months to drink the water that comes from this little fountain that was before us! Wow! Can you imagine?! The water was so special, so good that they made this very long drive. They were drinking it right on the spot! But for us Freys, we like cold water. So, we helped ourselves to the water from the fountain and then we waited awhile before we drank it as it was too warm. I think my dad would have loved to throw some ice cubes in there but that would have been diluting the healing qualities of the water. This is natural water by the way. It literally comes from the mountains from the hot springs, from inside the mountains. So, you don't need to filter the water. The water is all naturally filtered.

There are two places on the street corners where they have these fountains and anyone can go and get this water. As a matter of fact, they even have these jugs next to the fountains. It is amazing, but around the fountains it is almost like Hot Springs National Park becomes a gift-giving culture. Yes! Really! It is almost like a Santa convention where everyone takes these free jugs and fills them up with what is supposed to be the most wonderful water in the world! Kind of funny, but as I saw people taking these free jugs, the jugs began to look like candy canes as Hot Springs National Park took on the Christmas spirit! Hot Springs National Park, right before my very eyes, became a place filled with good will.

It was a happening place for me and very awe-inspiring for so many reasons. No doubt, The Hot Springs National Park was an unforgettable travel destination for me and my family. I think few can imagine visiting a place like this. My mom thought it was so wonderful she wanted to move there! I think I will always have an interest in visiting places like this because it is so different from the everyday places that we live and go to on a day-to-day basis.

I can honestly say that this is one of the best places to visit in the world! I loved the water and the experience. Good-bye Hot Springs National Park! I love your beautiful enchantment! I am thinking of something else Hot Springs National Park. You know, my mom makes the best croissant sandwiches with turkey and cheese. We also bring granola bars and munch them in the car. I'll bet your wonderful tasting water would be great to drink with my mom's number one amazing croissants! Yes! I don't think anything could better top off your fantastic water than my mom's croissant sandwiches! So long Hot Springs National Park! You are wonderful! This has been a great day everybody!

Your Friend Always,
Aida

GIVE ME A MICROSCOPE
I WANT TO KNOW
EVERYTHNG!

Aida Frey

GEORGE WASHINGTON CARVER NATIONAL MONUMENT

Diamond, Missouri

Hi Everybody,

The George Washington Carver National Monument is amazing. This place is amazing for so many reasons, but one in particular is it interprets George Washington Carver's life. It does such a great job that I really felt like I had met him by the time my parents and I left the Monument. I can't explain it. There is so much to know about this one person. He was so amazing.

I had an experience at this National Monument that I will never forget. I was filled with enthusiasm and curiosity. I wanted to learn more. I wanted to see everything. I think you cannot help but feel this way at The George Washington Carver National Monument because it was the way George Washington Carver was. He was so enthusiastic about nature and was referred to as the "Plant Doctor." He was an agricultural scientist and was born into slavery as a child. There was so much to him. What I really liked was he had a secret garden which he tended to as a kid. Called The Peanut Man, he was much more than that. George Washington Carver was a humanitarian and if you may remember, I spoke all about George Washington Carver in my book earlier and how he was a professor at Tuskegee.

I cannot help but mention again that George Washington Carver was called The Peanut Man because of his love for plants. He developed so many uses for the peanut. I just cannot get it out of my head all of the different uses of the peanut. So! Remember, as I mentioned earlier, the next time you eat sloppy joes with chili sauce or wash your hair with shampoo, remember George Washington Carver developed the use of the peanut in these products! Wow! And I thought that the peanut was just great for peanut butter and jelly sandwiches! See! I told you that you learn a lot at the George Washing Carver National Monument!

The one thing that really got to me when visiting the Monument was you really get to feel what he was about here. I remember my parents and I watched a movie all about him and then the rangers welcomed us and everyone was so friendly and introducing themselves. And then something really amazing happened! The Superintendent, who I call Mr. Jim, and his assistant Leslie stayed with us the entire day and I got to learn about the different uses of the peanut in a laboratory setting! It was just too amazing! It was one of the most amazing things that I have ever done. I got to put on a white laboratory coat and look in the microscope for hours. It was like I was in a lab and doing the research just like George Washington Carver did. It was the best experience. I just spent the whole day surrounded by microscopes wearing a lab coat! This was definitely not your everyday experience! It was a wonderful time for me! It was just such an awesome way for a kid to have a great day! Thank you Superintendent Jim and Leslie! Wow!

Your Friend Always,
Aida

SUPERINTENDENT JIM HEANEY
GEORGE WASHINGTON CARVER NATIONAL MONUMENT

Diamond, Missouri

Hello Aida!

So nice to be in your pages! I had a wonderful time with you at George Washington Carver National Monument. We are looking forward to your next visit! Well, let me tell you a little bit about myself as a kid, Aida! Okay! Where do I start? There is so much to tell!

Aida, as a kid, I had an interest in nature and animals, reptiles and amphibians in particular! I enjoyed hanging out playing in the woods and creeks, like all kids do. As I got older, however, my interests shifted towards history and literature - the compelling human stories of struggle and triumph such as those that speak to the founding of our nation, as well as the fight to end slavery and eventually secure Civil Rights. In literature, I enjoyed the literary works of Mark Twain, Stephen Crane and others. After graduating high school, I went to Temple University in Philadelphia where I majored in English and History. I think you and I definitely have a love of history in common!

After graduating from Temple, while looking for a job, I happened to tour the Edgar Allan Poe National Historical Site in Philadelphia. This is where the great Gothic poet and fiction writer lived and crafted some of his best work. The Park Ranger there gave us a captivating presentation which included touring the cellar which mirrored the setting for the murder scene in Poe's "The Black Cat." I was struck by what this Park Ranger was doing - connecting himself and others to this special place and stoking their curiosity to learn more. I decided this would be a very cool job for me!

Shortly after that visit to the Poe House, I decided to apply for a ranger position at Independence National Historical Park which is also in Philly. That's where many of the sites associated with the birth of our country are preserved such as the Liberty Bell and Independence Hall. I worked there for a summer, which was wonderful, and then took a job at the Poe House a year later. One of the really awesome things about the National Park Service is the opportunity to move around the country and experience new parks and cultures and share that knowledge with others. So I moved from Philadelphia to work at the historical park in Lowell, Massachusetts, then the beautiful antebellum town of Natchez, Mississippi and then to Ulysses S. Grant National Historic Site in St. Louis. After returning to Natchez for a few years, I moved on to Alabama where I worked with many Civil Rights veterans at the Selma to Montgomery National Historical Trail. It was a great honor to learn from living people who fought to secure voting rights - - - a rare opportunity to work with the actual history makers themselves!

After Selma, I accepted a job as Superintendent at George Washington Carver National Monument in Diamond, Missouri. This is where the renowned African American scientist, educator and humanitarian was born. I have enjoyed almost seven years here now. Do you know something, Aida? This place is filled with so many wonderful happenings! But, something else very special for me happened here Aida. George Washington Carver is where I met you and your wonderful family!

Aida, as the Superintendent, I am responsible for the overall park management - resource preservation and protection, budgeting, visitor services, partnership development, promoting the park, hiring, purchasing - and I work with a highly talented and dedicated group of about fifteen park employees, like Administrative Officer Leslie Sadler, to accomplish the work successfully. These days, we are very busy planning for the National Park Service Centennial in 2016. It will mark the 100th anniversary of the Organic Act that created the NPS, and the Centennial goal is to connect with the next generation of park visitors, supporters and advocates. So as much as we are celebrating a glorious past, we are also setting a stage for keeping the National Parks relevant for today's and tomorrow's youth. We are blessed to have young people like you Aida help us pass the torch to the next generation!

Aida, I was immediately struck by your dedication to the NPS when I first met you. We were the 150th park that you visited on your amazing 200 national park friendship tour! Of course you completed the Junior Ranger activity here, but I know you wanted to go beyond that and challenged the staff and myself with a lot of questions about Carver and the NPS as a whole. I was also struck with how deep and diverse your experiences and knowledge really were. You knew history, science, literature and had a great memory of every park you had visited. I am not sure how it came up in the conversation, but I remember we even discussed Greek and Roman mythologies! I was simply astounded with you then and now with having completed your 200 national parks journey and having a book written. I am so happy to be included in your pages! Aida, you probably have been to more parks than I have. I have been in this agency for over twenty years and here I was learning a lot about the parks from you!

Here at Carver's birthplace and childhood home, we interpret the young George and how he had an insatiable curiosity to learn about nature, science and art and the wonders of the Great Creator. Aida, you have that same thirst for knowledge at a very young age. When Carver left here, when he was about your age, maybe 12 or 13, he traveled throughout Missouri, Kansas and Iowa seeking education in high schools and colleges before moving on to Alabama and spending close to fifty years at Tuskegee Institute educating young people there. Aida, I do believe that you, too, have that same adventurous spirit as the young Carver in that you travel to learn more and share more. Now, of course, Carver as a black man in a white-dominated society faced incredible prejudice and even violence; he had to also overcome a tragic childhood - he never knew his father and his mother was apparently kidnapped and never returned. Aida, obviously you have advantages that Carver did not have. But one can see how someone like you could, in a sense, connect with, and be inspired by, the Carver story.

I also think, Aida, that you are inspired by all the stories you come across in your National Park travels and your personal tour! I am sure that you will, in turn, inspire others as well. You are an extraordinary young person and I really hope your dream of becoming a Park Ranger comes true. Aida, you have so much passion and so many experiences to offer to the next generation of park visitors, supporters and advocates. May you continue inspiring kids of your generation! You are someone who is an inspiration to us all!

LESLIE SADLER
GEORGE WASHINGTON CARVER NATIONAL MONUMENT

Diamond, Missouri

Hi Aida,

Surprise! Surprise! Leslie Sadler here!

Aida, I really enjoyed meeting you and I know you wanted to learn a bit more about me so here I am! When I was a kid, I didn't visit any national parks. I was the complete opposite of you. You see, The George Washing Carver National Monument was a school field trip for me and was the first national park I ever visited. It is really funny that I would end up working here! I must say that working for The George Washington Carver National Monument really fell in my lap. While studying at Missouri Southern State College in Joplin, I was asked to work as a temporary administrative clerk. I never left and was moved up to Administrative Officer.

You see, Aida, it is really very interesting how America's national parks attract many types of people. I am a person who was born to do administrative work. Not really an outdoors person, I love to play with papers. I guess you could call me a paper girl! Now, I know that has to sound funny to you, but it's the truth. But, it is also how I landed here at George Washington Carver where I grew to love the National Park Service and how I got to meet you and your family! You see, I was downstairs shuffling papers in my office when the phone rang and I heard this friendly voice on the other end and it was your dad! He was calling to set up your visit with us and I am so glad that he did!

Aida, I am so happy that I answered the phone the day your dad called. Your dad said he wanted to bring his daughter and wife to George Washington Carver and we spoke and speaking to him and meeting your mom and you was a great reminder of what I am doing here at The George Washington Carver National Monument. I am here to meet people like you and your family and help them learn about George Washington Carver.

Aida, I admire your interest in the National Parks at such a young age. I admire your huge love for history. And you know something else Aida, George Washington Carver ventured out on his own because he wanted to learn like you. To meet you was a big deal for me. I admire you and your family. You get out into the country and see what America is all about. Yes! I admire you, Aida. Keep following your passion, Aida! Keep loving America's national parks! And who knows Aida, we may see you as a director of the park service one day! Bravo Aida! You make America proud!

I may be compelled to face danger, but never fear it, and while our soldiers can stand and fight, I can stand and feed and nurse them.

Clara Barton

THE CLARA BARTON NATIONAL HISTORIC SITE

Glen Echo, Maryland

Hey Everybody,

The Clara Barton House was created in 1974 to talk about the life of Clara Barton. Clara Barton was an amazing woman in history. Wow! She was many things including a nurse, humanitarian and the founder of the American Red Cross which still exists today and where many people donate blood to help people who are in need.

I just have to talk about Clara Barton. She is such an inspiration and has such an amazing story! I visited the Clara Barton National Historic Site and the Clara Barton House in Maryland on our Washington, DC trip. It was awesome. Clara Barton was a woman that remains an inspiration for girls like me! Not only was she a nurse who founded the American Red Cross and one of the biggest humanitarians that the world has ever known, but she gives girls the feeling that we are important and we can be great leaders in life!

Let me tell you a little bit about Clarissa "Clara" Harlow Barton. She was born December 25, 1821 and died April 12, 1912. She preferred to be called Clara and remains one of the most honored and respected women in American history. Clara Barton dedicated her life to helping others in times of need both in America and abroad, in peacetime as well as during war. I found it very interesting that even as a child she always wanted to help others. As a child, Clara used to help injured pets. So! It is no wonder that she started The American Red Cross. And, when the Civil War started, she wanted to help the soldiers so she made bandages out of towels and sheets to be used on those soldiers who were wounded in action. She also asked people to help donate money to help the soldiers.

The Clara Barton Historic Site helps you understand so much about her. For me, I thought it was very interesting that Clara Barton (at a time when women were just not able to do much) got the okay, the permission form the War Department, to go to the front lines of the battlefields to care for the soldiers herself. Called the Angel of the Battlefield, she almost lost her life, but she continued to serve. She comforted the soldiers, bought and prepared food for them and searched for missing soldiers. In the years following the Civil War, she was able to reunite thousands of soldiers and their families. Interesting how this shy, small-town girl started the American Red Cross and was its president for twenty-three years.

I really liked Clara Barton's generosity and her desire to help humankind and animals. So, at school, when we had to dress up like someone famous in history that we admired, I remembered my Washington, DC trip. I must have raised my hand like one hundred times to the teacher to dress up like Clara Barton! She remains someone that I really think is amazing! And so, I dressed up like Clara Barton for my report at school.

The Clara Barton House is a gigantic house and is filled with love from the floor to the ceiling! Filled with bandages and blankets and medical supplies, The Clara Barton House also became the headquarters for The American Red Cross. Clara Barton also had many friends who lived there which is why you get the warm feeling of care and compassion in this house. You cannot help but feel that there was a goal to try to save people in The Clara Barton House. It is just amazing how Clara Barton was out there in the battlefields, showing the world how brave women are! Clearly Clara Barton was passionately compassionate about her fellow human beings, animals and life.

I feel like I am a bit like Clara Barton in regard to the fact that she always wanted to learn new things like me! And this is part of my fondness for America's National Parks because I get to learn so much when we visit them. The National Parks portray such a rich history and really make history come alive every time I visit! After visiting The

Clara Barton Historical Site, I could not help but pick Clara Barton for my report on someone famous!

Your Friend Always,
Aida

The White House is huge-
It is bigger than a hockey field!

Aida Frey

THE WHITE HOUSE
THE PRESIDENT OF THE UNITED STATES

1600 Pennsylvania Avenue NW
Washington, D.C.

Hey Everybody!

Let me tell you about my visit to probably one of the most famous places ever: The White House! Wow! Is it big?! You could put tons of hockey teams in there and not even bump into one another! It is enormous! I found something else very interesting. This location of the White House has been the home of every U.S. president since John Adams in 1800. It felt so awesome to know that all of these very important people in the United States had lived in this house where I was standing. I just couldn't stop thinking about it. I mean, just to think that so many important decisions were made by people who came through this place where I am well. I just couldn't get over this! Wow! It was just amazing.

The property is a National Heritage Site owned by the National Park Service and is part of the President's Park. It is painted white with the East Wing being used for receptions, parties and anything social. I just couldn't help but think how many balloons would fit in here! I understand that The White House receives 30,000 visitors a week. But, The White House is a very different kind of park and you can't just wake up one day and say I think I want to visit the White House. Oh no! It just doesn't work that way. I remember we had to plan six months ahead of time to go there. You really have to plan. My dad is very good at doing that. I remember he had to contact the federal senator from

Chicago in our particular situation six months ahead of time. So my dad contacted our representative from Chicago who is a representative to Washington, DC. He also filled out a form with a lot of questions. It seemed like he was up all night answering the questions. I began to understand during this process that The Secret Service has to approve you and they do this by checking everyone out that wants to visit The White House. It is very important for security reasons.

Visiting The White House is an experience. Everything about it is an experience. And you have no idea of its size until you are there. It is huge! I found myself constantly turning my head to try to see everything! While staring at The White House, I kept feeling that I was really staring at the symbol of our country. I am here where so many important decisions are made and so many important people work and visit. Yes! Seeing The White House is an experience! Let me tell you more about it.

First of all, it is not like you can just make a quick decision, get up one morning and say I think I will visit The White House today! Oh no! It takes planning and it takes lots and lots of planning! My dad made the arrangements for us. The Secret Service has to check you out. It is a process and everyone has to fill out this questionnaire and have a background check. There has to be enough space for you also. You are also told what day and time you can visit so you have to be very flexible to make everything work out.

The weather was cold as we boarded the train from Virginia to Washington, DC. It was cold and dark when we got off the subway. We made our way toward The White House. There was a huge line so other people got their okay for the same day we did. Now, there were lots of restrictions about what we could bring into The White House too. We brought our identifications. You must have an ID. No camera and no video were allowed. You could not bring baby strollers in the White House. We had to go through three check points to get through the door. It began to snow while we waited to go into The White House and it was freezing standing in line. They have to check tickets and IDs before you step into the White House, too. Security will make sure that you do not have cameras or food or drinks. Really, you can only bring yourself, your tickets and IDs. I was happy once we got past the first check point which are x-ray machines and mental detectors; German Shepherds make great police dogs and they are sniffing too! There are professionally trained bomb dogs also! Everyone standing in line is excited to go into The White House. You can just feel it! The line is all happy!

We were on our own once inside. We were directed where we could go but we could spend as much time as we wanted. We saw the blue room, the green room and the red room; we saw dining rooms where queens and heads of states are entertained. There is a painting of George Washington there with a really interesting story about it. When the British attacked The United States in 1812 for the second time, Dolly Madison, who was the first lady at the time, did something that was so amazing. The British started burning down The White House and Dolly Madison was trying to save everything she could from being burned. She was married to James Madison. Going around the White House while it was being attacked she tried to save things. She wanted to save things that were historical and one of them was the famous painting of George Washington. Wow!

You can only visit the rooms on the first floor of The White House. It is very interesting that the presidents saved the old pieces of furniture. It is a self- guided tour. You read about what happened in the room and why it is famous. There are people in each room that can answer your questions. It is an amazing feeling to be in The White House. You have a different person in each room giving you the history and telling you the famous stuff that has gone on. Each room has a story. One room we visited was where Lady Diana danced with President Reagan. There are historical signs everywhere to tell you what you are seeing. It is so nice to be in there. The hallways are very large and very tall. You can look out of the windows and see the rose garden. It is very awesome. You just get a nice feeling. I looked outside and saw the first dog. There was a secret service guy taking the dog out. There just was something amazing about seeing the first dog! My parents got excited as well as other people touring The White House. Everyone really got excited about seeing the first dog! Wow! And Beau is the name of the dog. It was a very special feeling.

So remember, if you want to visit The White House, you have to call way ahead of time. It is not a spontaneous visit. We were waiting outside in freezing weather but it was worth it just to be inside this famous place in history! It is such a nice feeling. You know that all the presidents lived there except for Washington because The White House wasn't done when he was president. So it all starts with John Adams being the first president in The White House. It is just an amazing feeling to be in a place where our presidents have been!

Everything looks great in the White House. I mean, to me, it all looks perfect. Everything is so shiny and polished. They were taking the pieces of the chandelier off and cleaning them by hand when we were there. It was really interesting. I mean even the simplest of things seem mesmerizing when you are in The White House. There are people coming and going and you don't know who they are but there is always someone cleaning something or helping you find someplace. You are never alone in The White House. There is a lot of stuff going on! It is a very busy place and I was just trying to take it all in.

It is really a presidential feeling to be in The White House. You can't really explain it, but you just have to experiences it. Being there and being part of their living quarters for the day is a really cool atmosphere. I must say that I really loved it and I can't wait to go back there again. And so, it was toward the end of our time there and we were on the way out when I saw there were some fancy baskets with paper in them. We looked at it and it was a recipe from President Obama's wife, a pizza recipe on how to make a veggie pizza. So, that was kind of interesting. It was interesting because it was fancy in a basket. Once you step outside the door of The White House you are done. You have to understand, you definitely can't go back inside. The doors are closed to you. You see the marines standing there and you exit on the driveway with this wonderful feeling that you have been in a very important place!

There is nothing like
having your own day!

Aida Frey

EFFIGY MOUNDS NATIONAL MONUMENT
AIDA DAY

APRIL 18th, 2015

Hey Everybody,

My second visit to Effigy Mounds was so wonderful. My parents and I got up early! This was a very special day. It was Aida Day at Effigy Mounds! Yes! Not too often a kid has a day reserved just for her! But, that's what happened to me! April 18th, 2015 was proclaimed Aida Day at Effigy Mounds and it was a milestone in my life!

So, my parents and I got up very early that morning. I believe it was 6 in the morning. It may have even been earlier. It would be my second time at Effigy Mounds and my first and only Junior Ranger Aida Frey Day! This was indeed a celebration. Zigzagging our way to Effigy Mounds, four hours from Chicago, we are one excited car! Now, this time we have GPS as opposed to four years earlier when we didn't have it. I am fourteen years old now. And as we arrive at Effigy Mounds and I meet Jim, the Superintendent, I am wearing my vest filled with medals and more medals! I don't have Tom with me this time but I have many pins, medals and badges. I have my hat on. It is so cool! Superintendent Jim and I shake hands and I meet Albert who closely works with him. It was such a wonderful welcome!

They had a big cake waiting for me in the Visitors Center. There were many rangers present and others congratulating me on my journey of accomplishment! I was congratulated and applauded for visiting two hundred of America's national parks in four years! Albert and

Jim brought spears out and they taught me how to throw a spear in this huge grassy area. It was awesome! I had such a great time! It is always wonderful at the national parks to learn something new! I learned that the spears relate back to when the American Indians were at the Mounds. Spears were very important. They demonstrated the importance of the spear and the American Indian. I threw the spear many times and was quite good.

Four years later at Effigy Mounds, I am now a Junior Ranger of patches and pins and badges and medals. I am Junior Ranger Aida Frey and I am presented with a wood plaque for my accomplishments! I am really just very proud of myself that I have made it to 200 parks in four years and that I have a day to call my own! Wow!

You can't resist nature at Effigy Mounds. It is so beautiful, so scenic. It is just so pretty. But the mounds are almost like your hiking buddies. They are there waiting for you, no matter how long it takes you to reach them. They become like old friends, welcoming you and waiting for you to come back for another visit. Effigy Mounds is where I first established my relationship with nature. Far from highways and shopping malls, I became a different person learning what I think about different things. I like seeing the birds and flowers and trees like this. It is so different to be out here in this rugged wilderness. There is no boredom out here, just beauty; I wonder if the trees and birds even notice me. There is a spirit in nature that I found at Effigy Mounds on my second trip here. Effigy Mounds is so beautiful that I found it difficult to snap photos. I just wanted to admire it every minute. Visiting Effigy Mounds and seeing it and hiking is so different than just seeing the caterpillars in your backyard or a butterfly landing on your garden hose. Effigy Mounds for me as a nine-year- old and as a fourteen-year-old is like one big humongous grassy yard with the most beautiful leaves and trees you have ever seen!

Thank you Effigy Mounds for your inspiration. I will never forget my journey to the top! I couldn't have dreamed of anything better. You were the first national park I ever experienced. And it was such a positive experience that I was inspired to begin my journey of 200 National Parks in four years and I accomplished it! But, I began my journey because of my love for America's national parks which began on my first visit to my first park, Effigy Mounds! Thank you Effigy Mounds! I can't wait to come back! Thank you for giving me Aida Day! It was perfect!

I would just like to say that I am a kid looking back at being a kid. This was my second visit to Effigy Mounds. I saw it differently than when I was a nine-year-old. Of course, it was still the pretty way I remembered it, but it was filled with so much more meaning on my second visit. The mounds are so unique, the views are ever more spectacular. And, of course, this time at Effigy Mounds, I am a Super Junior Ranger with a vest of badges and pins and sashes from my tour of 200 National Parks. But it all began here at Effigy Mounds which was the first national park that I ever visited!

I would like to just stay at Effigy Mounds and play in the leaves! I love this place!

Your Friend Always,
Aida

ALBERT LEBEAU
CHIEF OF CULTURAL RESOURCES PROGRAM
EFFIGY MOUNDS NATIONAL MONUMENT

Hi Aida~

It is your friend Albert LeBeau from Effigy Mounds. Thanks for asking me to step into your pages. I am so happy to be here. Well, a bit about me.

My icons were my parents. They were the first ones from my reservation to receive college degrees. I grew up, Aida, with a sense of education and hero worship for my mom and dad and just knowing something big was on my horizon. You see, Aida, because of my parents and their support, I never forgot where I came from which is the Cheyenne River Sioux Tribe. Our ancestors were warriors. They fought in The Little Big Horn Battle. Many ancestors were killed at Wounded Knee. I know you love history, Aida. I am related to Standing Bear and I am the great great great nephew of Luther Standing Bear who was an author in the late 1800s and early 1900s. He wrote stories that have been told for generations.

I like the simple world and sometimes I just want to jump on a horse and be a cowboy and not have anyone around me! I don't need to have anyone around me, Aida. I don't need a cell phone or video games. It is nice, of course, to have conveniences but I know how to live without them. Sitting Bull states "Take the good things from the whites and leave the bad. Make your life easier. Leave the bad stuff."

I spend at least an hour to two hours every day at The Visitor Center at Effigy Mounds. I answer questions anyone visiting may have. I will talk to specific tribal groups and try to answer their questions as well. I practice my traditions, one of which is a pipe carrier. This means I cannot drink and I cannot have blood on my hands. I try to be a good pipe carrier and I try to be a good man, a good person. I don't talk about myself and I am here to help my tribe and my family and my country. I do this for those who cannot speak anymore, those who have passed on. Aida, this is what has taken me to Effigy Mounds. I like the Native American preservation at Effigy Mounds and the way the Mounds are kept and honored.

I have learned to walk in two worlds. I walk with my humor and tease my friends and myself; teasing is a form of adoration in my culture. Teasing is part of Indian humor. It is part of our historic drama and our own personal drama; it is what it is and what we laugh about. For example, Aida, Native American funerals are hilarious. They are half laughing and half crying. We all go home eventually. My home is South Dakota. I am part of an extended family which is medium-sized. When my family gets together, there are usually around 400 of us attending. A large family gathering is 500 to 1,000 people.

Aida, you have to be able to take people the way they are. You should be very proud of what you have done at such a young age. You give me hope for the future. You love history. You are a combination of tree-hugging and nature embracing. Your book is a thoughtful journey into the life of a kid and her country! I love that!

SUPERINTENDENT JIM NEPSTAD
EFFIGY MOUNDS NATIONAL PARK

Aida,

I am so happy to be in your pages! Wow! And, guess what?! I love the National Parks too! I fell in love with America's national parks at a very young age. I vacationed as a child to America's National Parks like you! Yes! I come from a National Park loving family just like you. I have always been smitten with Yellowstone by the way! I am so taken in by various geysers (Old Faithful being one of them) and infrequently erupting ones.

I grew up in Onalaska, Wisconsin. My first job was providing cave tours at Wind Cave National Park in South Dakota. It was a seasonal job that I took in between college. I never believed I was lucky enough to work for America's national parks and so I was thrilled about doing this. I know how much you love caves and that you used to be afraid of them but now you even feel safe in them! Well, I share your love for caves and I am going to tell you, Aida, I have been obsessed with caves since I was a little kid!

So Aida, my first permanent position was Mammoth Cave National Park in Kentucky. The cave world is a very exciting one! Walking in big passages, squeezing through and up and down the obstacle courses caves present, I enjoyed exploring the unexplored passages that I found exciting. Exploring the modern world is a thrill. You don't know what is over the next hill in cave exploration. Caves completely dark hundreds of feet underground, miles from an entrance, delicate crystal formations mapping what is found always presented the potential for getting lost, but I never did.

I moved to Apostle Islands for twelve years and then to Effigy Mounds, the national park of animal-shaped mounds and the most spectacular view of the Mississippi River Valley you will ever see! Effigy Mounds shoots the thought that Iowa is just cornfields, Aida! The American Indians shaped the land and appreciated it. The mounds are in the shape of animals and are very life-like and have been there over a thousand years. It is interesting that they are still here! The Mounds are the reason Effigy Mounds is here! It is the reason the national park is here! It is what makes Effigy Mounds so unique. And Aida, we work closely with the tribes that are descended from the folks who constructed the mounds and this is what Effigy is all about! Yes, Aida, there is history here! There is history everywhere!

JIM AND ALBERT
EFFIGY MOUNDS NATIONAL MONUMENT

Aida,

Albert and Jim here!

We both just wanted to come back into your pages just for a second to tell you that we wanted to do something special for you to commemorate your second visit to Effigy Mounds and to salute your 200 National Park Journey in four years! How exciting this must be for you and we are excited for you at accomplishing this! So, we began to think of the different things that we could do for you to commemorate such a wonderful occasion! And, we came up with giving you your own day at Effigy Mounds!

We feel that you are a special person to us, Aida, and that you are a dear friend to us as well. You are thought of very highly at Effigy Mounds, Aida! And to think that your 200 park journey started with Effigy Mounds! And so, a special thanks to a special person, we have given you, on behalf of us both, Aida Day at Effigy Mounds! Congratulations, Aida!

ALLEGHANY PORTAGE RAILROAD NATIONAL HISTORIC SITE
MEGAN O'MALLY

Hi Aida! It is Megan O'Mally! Thank you for inviting me into your pages. So nice to be here! Well, your wonderful book opens with your two-gun salute at Allegheny and I just wanted to step into your pages and say Aida, it is such a pleasure to know you! You are a great kid! So, a little bit about the person who was part of the planning of your two-gun salute!

Well, I grew up in the suburbs of Pittsburgh. I did not visit many parks as a kid like you. Aida, I didn't visit my first national park until high school. My brother worked for the national parks and it was really through him that I developed a love for them and it was through him that I began to visit them. The Florida Everglades was my first national park, Aida. I remember it well. I was a freshman in high school and it was such a unique experience for me. I found The Everglades so unique and so exciting that I kept thinking about it over and over again!

So Aida, that is how I got my start and began loving America's national parks! I am Chief of Interpretation at Allegheny Portage Railroad National Historical Site and it was my pleasure to coordinate and come up with your 2- gun salute! We wanted to make your 200th park a special thing, a very special thing. We thought very hard how to recognize the occasion. And I want you to know that it was the first time in the park's history to do a 2-gun salute, a special black power 2-gun salute! On behalf of Alleghany Portage Railroad National Historic Site, we want to thank you for your dedication. You are so accomplished at such a young age. Oh, one more thing. I am quite struck by what a great kid you are, Aida! And we just want to let you know that you are so much fun to talk to!

SUPERINTENDENT DAVE RUTH
RICHMOND NATIONAL BATTLEFIELD PARK
MAGGIE WALKER NATIONAL HISTORIC SITE

Richmond, Virginia

Aida your story is intriguing. I just found myself sitting down and talking to you and just really taken in on your thirst for knowledge. I really enjoyed shooting your video with you wearing your junior ranger hat and vest with your sashes and pins and medals. It is no wonder that you are the talk of the town! I felt as if we were launching you with the news and media with this video! As a matter of fact when we were rolling the video about you I just said stop rolling everyone. I just wanted to talk to you.

Aida you are a very interesting person. Your interest in America's national parks is beyond inspirational. It is mesmerizing! I found myself completely taken in by your interests and your enthusiasm. You are one great kid! And just like your parents are taking you to America's national parks and learning and experiencing history, my grandfather and my father took me to Gettysburg when I was eight years and that's when I became totally enamored by the story of the Civil War!

Now, I guess a little bit more about me. I grew up in a small Pennsylvania town where everyone was interested in the past. My grandfather and my father took me to Gettysburg. I was eight years old at the time. I was totally enamored by the story of the Civil War. I spent endless hours paging through Civil War photographs. I could spend hours and hours reading about The Civil War.

Hooked on history and understanding America's past I went through high school expanding this interest of mine and I became a reenactor. I actually became a Civil War battle reenactor! I felt a connection to America's national parks during a battle reenactment in Pennsylvania. I guess you could say I am a living history interpreter! I interviewed with America's national parks service in Fredericksburg on the battlefield in Virginia. It was a summer job. I was shown where my tent was and where my bale of hay was for bedding. I cooked on an open fire and I was smitten with it all!

I am the Superintendent of The Richmond National Battlefield Park and The Maggie Walker National Historic Site. It is a great place to work. It is a place where we are reminded to follow our dreams! Remember to follow your dreams, Aida! You have an exceptional story here. You are the hidden gem of America's National Park Service!

Twas, the night before Christmas,
And out in the streets,
Children were running all over Germany
In their bare feet;
And in front of their houses,
They left their Christmas clues by the twos,
For St. Nicholas was coming
To stuff sugar pretzels and chocolates in their boots and their shoes!

RANGER REGGIE MURRAY

William Howard Taft National Historic Site
Cincinnati, Ohio

Dear Aida,

Reggie Murray here! So happy to be in your pages!

I was born in Alabama, my father was in the military. As a kid I travelled around the world twice. And just as your adventures to America's national parks began when you were nine years old, my adventures in Europe began at nine years old. I saw my first International National Park in Germany at nine years old. I lived across the street from it. The name of the town was Bruch.

I definitely talk about my childhood with a glimmer, Aida. You see, as a kid I travelled around the world twice and it was in Europe when I learned about cultures and castles and saw enormous drawbridges! It is where I learned about St. Nicolaus and it is where I left my shoes out on the front porch so St. Nicolaus would put chocolate in them!

Aida you are a special person. When you and your family arrived at William Howard Taft National Historic Site you were proudly wearing your Jr. Ranger gear complete with badges and Ranger hat. You had patches and badges from so many of America's national parks. I remember I asked you what you wanted to be when you grow up and become an adult and you said that you wanted to be a park ranger! Well Aida, it was at this point you just won my heart as a young woman starting early in life visiting and immersing yourself in the wonderful resources of the National Park Service.

Aida, you are a bright and smart young lady and my life as a Park Ranger was very much touched when you earned your Junior Ranger badge from the William Howard Taft NHS. I then was called again into service but this time as a Buffalo Soldier. This time I met you, Aida, at the Charles Young Buffalo Soldier National Monument. I felt that you deserved the opportunity to be sworn in as the first Junior Ranger of the Charles Young Buffalo Soldier National Monument by a Buffalo Soldier Costumed interpreter. So Sgt. Reginald B. Murray of the fighting 10th Cavalry, of the Buffalo Soldier Regiment rode 1 ½ hours to meet and swear you in, Ms. Aida Frey, in as an official Junior Ranger of the Charles Young Site.

Aida you are an inspiration to all. Whenever I get the chance I bring out your picture and show other kids why the national parks are important to some people like you, Aida Frey. You are Junior Ranger extraordinary in my book! Keep up your goals and be the best Junior Ranger you can be and thank you for asking me to step into your pages! I have had a great time!

CHARLES YOUNG BUFFALO SOLDIERS NATIONAL MONUMENT

Ohio

Dear Reggie,

I want to thank you for driving to see me at the Charles Young Buffalo Soldiers National Monument in Ohio. It was a thrill for me to be the first Junior Ranger in this monument. I still have the beautiful Junior Ranger certificate that you gave me framed! It is so awesome!

I like that you and I love history! I loved learning that the Buffalo Soldiers patrolled and protected the national parks out in the west. The Buffalo Soldiers were brave and they were just so cool! I really enjoyed hearing you talk about history and military history. I can't wait to come back here again! I want to tell you that after seeing you at the Charles Young Buffalo Soldiers National Monument, I love history even more (if that is possible) and I love military history!

Thank you so much for coming into my pages and for coming into my life! You are such a cool Ranger and I agree with you that the Buffalo Soldiers were everybody's soldiers!

Aida

I think being outside in nature
Just makes everyone
feel like a kid!

Aida Frey

WENDY DAVIS

HARPERS FERRY NATIONAL HISTORICAL PARK
Harpers Ferry, West Virginia

Aida,

Wendy Davis Here! It is so nice of you to include me in your pages. I am so happy to be here and so happy to know you! Aida, you are what the Junior Ranger Program is all about! You are a great person, Aida, and you are a hero to so many kids all over the country! I would have been heartbroken if I had missed the opportunity to be in your pages! You are, indeed, very special not only to me but to America's national parks!

Aida, you and your family have tied in the family experience with America's national parks. You are the vision! You see, Aida, the light goes on in the parks. The best experience is just what you are doing! You are visiting America's national parks and you are getting the entire experience of what the national parks are all about. Of course, each park is very different from the next park but that is the story of history. The national parks are what it is all about. It is where history and present-day life comes together!

I admire your love for history and your desire to learn what is behind America's national parks and what is involved in preserving them and their history! You and your family are seeing America's most monumental sights! Your courage and bravery is beautiful and is reflected in your travels to America's national Parks. I admire you Aida! You are doing something that you love and you are interested in America's national parks from so many different perspectives. You and your parents are fabulous and all of you are so supportive of one another and that's what really makes your visits to the national parks so amazing and so beautiful! You are the experience, Aida!

Aida, I grew up in Washington State. I loved the outdoors as a kid. Visiting my family's history was a wonderful thing for me as a child. My mother's grandfather attended a one room school house in the North Cascades National Park in Central Washington. I loved going there and hiking and gardening and looking at the ground and seeing plants and animals. Aida, I stayed outside until the streetlights came on! I just love being outside.

Thank you Aida for helping make the Junior Ranger Program come alive in the most wonderful of ways with your devotion! It is indeed a pleasure to know you and your family!

"Wilderness is a necessity ... They will see what I
meant in time. There must be places for human beings to satisfy their
souls. Food and drink is not all. There is the spiritual. In
some it is only a germ, of course, but the germ will
grow." "Everybody needs beauty as well as bread,
places to play in and pray in, where nature may heal and
give strength to body and soul."
"How hard to realize that every camp of men
or beast has this glorious starry firmament for a roof. In
such places, standing alone on the mountaintop, it is easy
to realize that whatever special nests we make —
leaves and moss like the marmots and the birds, or tents or
piled stone — we all dwell in a house of one room
— the world with the firmament for its roof —
and are sailing the celestial spaces without leaving
track."
"The mountains are fountains of men as well
as of rivers, of glaciers, of fertile soil. The great poets,
philosophers, prophets, able men whose thoughts and deeds
have moved the world, have come down from the mountains
— mountain-dwellers who have grown strong there with
the forest trees in Nature's work-shops. –

John Muir Founder---The Sierra Club

JON JARVIS

Jon Jarvis has served with the National Park Service for 39 years as ranger, biologist, superintendent and regional director throughout the western US and Alaska. In 2009, he was appointed the 18th director.

Aida, you inspire me. You inspire me through your travels of America's national parks. You penetrate the deeper meaning behind the places that you visit. America's national parks are more than beautiful; they are filled with stories that represent passion. You have a personal connection with America's national parks just like they have a personal connection with history. The national parks are inspirational, Aida! We tend to well up with the values that they have carried with them for centuries.

Aida, I love the outdoors. I grew up in the Shenandoah Valley in Virginia in the country. My home backed up against the national forest. Dashing out of the house, I was an outdoorsy kind of kid who loved to catch insects! And I will have you know, Aida, it was the norm for me to bring home snakes, lizards, frogs and more for my bedroom terrarium! Hair aflutter, accompanied by my pack of fifteen raw-boned hounds and baying beagles, I would vanish off into those precious seconds and run wild in the woods until my shadows gave way to the forest.

From the colorful flutters of a butterfly, to the wingless spider crawling in the sunlight, I would not crack a twig and clear my own little space in the forest to think. And it was here that I would experience my thoughts, realize my love for science and nourish my respect for nature.

Little did I know that I was experiencing what would later become known as a prescription for the outdoors and a big part of my career as America's 18th National Parks Director!

I would like to tell you a bit more about this Aida. When I graduated college in 1975, I pursued a dream to travel to the great parks of the west. So, in the fall of 1975, I outfitted a 1968 GMC van as a camper and travelled to many of the great national parks such as Yellowstone, Glacier, Olympic and Redwood. I was in awe of these amazing places. It was on this trip I had my first "ranger" experience. I was sitting in a Yellowstone campground and watching as a camper next to me tried to start his campfire by dumping gasoline on a pile of logs he had just bucked up with a chainsaw. He soon had his entire campsite on fire. Well Aida, I pulled a shovel out of my van, calmly walked over and scratched a line in the duff around his campsite and let it burn out.

I arrived back on the east coast in the late winter without much money and stayed at my brother's house in Alexandria, VA. While looking for a job, my brother handed me a Draft Environmental Impact Statement to review for him since he was working as an environmental lobbyist. Aida, I really do think it was at this moment that all of the early influences came together: a love of the outdoors, a concern about the threats facing our national parks, a public service inspired by my parents, an activist big brother and a science education. Here was a possibility of a career with the National Park Service, an institution that aligned with my values. A few months later, I was hired as a GS-4-026 Park Technician at the Bicentennial Information Center in Washington, DC. Now Aida, it was a long way from Yellowstone, but I loved the job and the people with whom I worked. One of the other seasonals I met that summer was a beautiful woman named Paula, now my wife of 34 years! The nation's Bicentennial in 1976 and the NPS Centennial in 2016 will bookend my 40 years in the NPS. Over that time, Paula and I have raised a family, moved nine times, lived in Mission 66 housing and made lifelong friends in the NPS family.

Each of us in the NPS has those moments when we know we have made the right decision with our career, our lives. It can be an encounter with a visitor, especially children, whose curiosity and wonder are ignited by our skill at showing them the natural world. It can be standing in a place in history, on the bloody fields of the Civil War or at Thomas Jefferson's desk and feel the chill of being in the spot that shaped our country. I know that you know what I am feeling here Aida. It is about making history come alive! Yes! It can be on the edge of an arroyo with the canyon wren trilling as the sun settles into the desert. It can be in a mountain forest where the only sound is the soft shush of falling snow flakes. These moments accumulate in us Aida; they give us strength, they reinforce our resolve that these parks need us. They need our passion, our commitment to their preservation for the enjoyment of future generations. They certainly do for me.

I think I get my appreciation for the outdoors from my dad. The outdoor is rejuvenating Aida! It is the sunshine, the rain, the clouds and the stars! There is nothing like it! Aida, to experience little things like the leaves crunching under your feet or to feel the playfulness of the breeze ruffling the trees - - - Well, it is just nature at its very best! What a fun gift the punch of color is in America's national parks! Everything is just so beautiful!

"Hello" is somehow easier to say in America's national parks than if you were out in the street. Perhaps this is because we feel with our hearts in America's national parks Aida. Everywhere you turn is friendship! Yes! We feel with our hearts. You become part of the family of America's national parks when you visit. Aida, you are definitely part of this family! May you visit often!

I am many stories, Aida. I would give anything to be that little boy again darting out of the house, running after the clouds, catching insects and disappearing off into the woods! That little boy, undoubtedly, will always make me smile!

Thank you for asking me to be part of your pages, Aida. You are our Little Ambassador. It is an honor to be your friend!

Kids do a lot of thinking
But the world doesn't realize this.
That is why kids need a rest
stop in their life
Where they can just rest
and think!

Aida Frey

REST STOP STORY

Hey Everybody,

I want to close my book with this rest stop story!

Now, I have seen incredible waterfalls and have been on roads where I have been swallowed up by gigantic forests. I have travelled side roads that have taken me back in time to battlefields and military parks. I have wound around mountains and have seen sunsets and sunrises and the beautiful colors of fall and walked through dew-drenched leaves. I have seen wildlife so close I could reach out and touch them. I have been in old cottage homes, boyhood towns and seen the coolest things that you could ever imagine. But, my story would not be complete if I didn't talk about this rest stop adventure.

It was one of our roadside pull-offs along I-57 along the Indiana border. The road bumped under me as we came to this wonderful stopping place. I remember I was ten years old and the car windows in the back were all the way down splashing me with sunlight. I couldn't wait to get out and stretch my legs. The wind felt warm upon my face. I like when my dad drives and I have my windows down. It makes me smile!

We had been in the car for quite a bit when we came across this rest stop that was tucked in the trees. It half-disappeared into the countryside. It was almost like a hideaway that you thought at first you just may have imagined. I thought it was some kind of astonishing secret!

Some roadside pull-offs have playgrounds and park-like areas and other kids playing. In this particular rest stop, there weren't any other kids and I was by myself; of course, my parents were with me. I remember getting out of the car and running around and how this rest area gave me space to let my energy out from the drive. My dad grabbed the football we always brought along with us to throw back and forth at rest stops. Really, I would have preferred to play hockey but it is kind of hard to play hockey at a rest area.

At the rest stops I always read the signs where they have information on the state that we are visiting. I also always go to the vending machines and get snacks. I didn't do either at this rest stop. I don't know why. I just stood underneath the shade enjoying my own little corner of the world thinking about my two hundred park tour and my badges and pins and sashes. I was remembering something very special to me and that was my cherry blossom badge.

The National Mall in Washington, DC covers a lot of national parks. I was very fortunate that on our Washington, DC trip we were there during cherry blossom time. The cherry blossoms were out. We were there and very fortunate. I had all sorts of questions as to when they planted the trees. The cherry blossom badge is a very unique badge and it is only given out one month a year and that is during cherry blossom season.

The cherry blossom season brings nature into the city of DC. If you go back in history, cherry blossoms were presented to Washington, DC by the Japanese. The city becomes a pinkish/whitish world during cherry blossom season and it is so beautiful. I picked a couple of the cherry blossoms up. Wow! They were like flower petals and were so very soft and precious. I couldn't take my eyes off of the cherry trees that lined the area around the Thomas Jefferson Memorial as well as the walkways dotted with cherry trees that lined the Franklin Delano Roosevelt Memorial.

I think about nature and the beauty of the outdoors and I look around at the rest stop. This one rest stop along I-57 is definitely a rest stop for birds and butterflies, I think. It was so pretty and I remember just watching the butterflies flying in the sunshine and the birds dotting the sky and I am taken back to the pinkish/whitish world of the flowering cherry trees in Washington, DC that seem to hug the sky and give me my beautiful cherry blossom badge.

See Ya,

Aida

My Book Has Taken Us
To So Many Awesome Places
Thank You So Much For Coming!

Aida Frey

EPILOGUE

Sometimes, I feel like I want to pack up all of my belongings and stash them in my parent's white Chevy Impala and just be a kid traveler and travel the country. I feel like I want to just spend my life observing and looking at the homes built on Lookout Mountain and see the black bears and wolves with their never-to-be-forgotten visits to the park tables looking for food wondering why in the world we are snapping pictures of them! Of course, the dream of this kind of life takes me away from hockey and my high school friends and their birthday parties not to mention my concert going.

I am a traveler! But I am a lot more. I am a collection of fun and entertaining stories! Of course, the absence of my mom's home baked chocolate chip cookies when we are on the road seems to really be having an effect on my life! Yep! I would love to be eye-to-eye with a chunk of my mom's home baked chocolate chips right about now. On the other hand, the absence of asparagus has little effect on me. My dad and I are the cookie monsters at home by the way. We finish them in one day. We eat all the cookies that are in sight!

I am really glad that my family and I go by car. The car gives a kid a lot of time to figure stuff out. I mean, you can think about the teachers you have, the friends you've made, your phone conversations and the music selections you've downloaded for your trip. Now, of course, my parents are talking back-and-forth non-stop in the front seat. My dad is the driver and my mom is the navigator. Every now and then I poke my head in the front seat and make sure they are okay.

I like travelling because I get to see so much but I also like spending time with my family. You see, when I am at home with my family we are all doing our own stuff. But when I am travelling with my family, we are together all the time. We are all in the car or in the motel room. Everything is family time and it is like we are not only family but we are friends. It is really kind of cool.

Writing "hi" on my feet and putting them on the window and popping vampire teeth in my mouth is just fun stuff I like doing while on the road. It is entertaining and are some of my favorite things to do when I travel. There is no privacy when you travel. Sometimes we are all brushing our teeth at the same time! Sometimes it is annoying especially if we are on the road for three weeks, but it is my family so who cares! You know, nothing is perfect in life, but I think that the national parks come as close to being perfect as you can get and there is nothing more perfect than a kid leaning against the trees!

Thanks for coming everybody! I have had so much fun! Wow! :-)

Your Friend Always,
Aida

ABOUT THE AUTHOR

Aida Frey's home base is in Algonquin, Illinois.